I0762761

Grounded Living

GROUNDED

LIVING

HARMONIZING DESIGN AND NATURE IN THE HOME

Anita Yokota

Photographs by Sara Ligorria-Tramp

CLARKSON POTTER / PUBLISHERS
New York

Clarkson Potter/Publishers
An imprint of the Crown Publishing Group
A division of Penguin Random House LLC
1745 Broadway
New York, NY 10019
clarksonpotter.com
penguinrandomhouse.com

Photography credits appear on page 267.

Library of Congress Cataloging-in-Publication Data
Names: Yokota, Anita author | Ligorria-Tramp, Sara photographer
Title: Grounded living / Anita Yokota ; photographs by Sara Ligorria-Tramp. Identifiers: LCCN 2025013302 (print) | LCCN 2025013303 (ebook) | ISBN 9798217033829 hardcover | ISBN 9798217033836 ebook | Subjects: LCSH: Interior decoration—Environmental aspects
Classification: LCC NK2113 .Y65 2026 (print) | LCC NK2113 (ebook) | DDC 747—dc23/eng/20250625
LC record available at https://lccn.loc.gov/2025013302
LC ebook record available at https://lccn.loc.gov/2025013303

ISBN 979-8-217-03382-9
Ebook ISBN 979-8-217-03383-6

Editor: Angelin Adams
Editorial assistant: Darian Keels
Designer: Marysarah Quinn
Production editor: Natalie Blachere
Production: Jessica Heim
Compositors: Merri Ann Morrell and Hannah Hunt
Copy editor: Eldes Tran
Proofreaders: Rachel Holzman and Miriam Taveras
Indexer: Elise Hess
Publicist: Lauren Chung
Marketer: Andrea Portanova

Manufactured in China

10 9 8 7 6 5 4 3 2 1

First Edition

The authorized representative in the EU for product safety and compliance is Penguin Random House Ireland, Morrison Chambers, 32 Nassau Street, Dublin D02 YH68, Ireland, https://eu-contact.penguin.ie

For my
Rachel, Emily, and Natalie,
never forget Thoreau's words:
"Go confidently in the direction
of your dreams. Live the life
you have imagined."

Contents

Biophilia at Home

What if your home could do more than just shelter you? What if it could also heal you? As a licensed therapist for twenty years and an interior designer of nearly fifteen years, I have noticed a common thread running through all my clients' lives: the constant hustle and bustle—the racing, juggling, and striving that often leaves little time to simply breathe and be in the one place where we're most comfortable. At home. Finding refuge within our own homes these days isn't just a luxury, it's essential to our well-being.

When life feels overwhelming, many of us turn to nature without even realizing it. We step outside for a breath of fresh air, take the dog for a walk, or simply gaze at the horizon to reset ourselves. Nature in its simplicity offers a kind of therapy that no app or gadget can replicate. That's the power of biophilia, a design philosophy that promotes bringing the healing qualities of the natural world into our everyday spaces.

I've always been drawn to natural elements in design—floral wallpaper, cascading greenery, woven textures—but I didn't have the vocabulary to explain why they felt so right. Over time, I've realized it's not just about aesthetics; it's about creating spaces that feel alive, that breathe, and that connect us to the earth.

Infuse your interior with sunlight, natural materials, greenery, and more to bring the benefits we get from the outdoors inside.

RYAN HOLIDAY
THE DAILY STOIC

Nature may not always be perfect, and that is its beauty. Stones are rough, leaves are asymmetrical, and even the most vibrant gardens have bare patches where plants don't take root. But in those imperfections, there's peace, resilience, and renewal. That's the same beauty we can invite into our homes—a beauty that not only enhances the way our spaces look, but also transforms how we feel in them.

Biophilic design is about choosing decor and rituals that give us a sense of place—grounding elements, if you will. My goal with this book is to help you create your safe space. Because when we feel safe, our mind automatically relaxes, our cortisol levels go down, and our dopamine and serotonin levels rise.

To create this book, I went searching for some of the best examples of biophilic design by interior designers around the world (be sure to flip to page 267 to see who designed which rooms). In these pages, we will explore just how nature-inspired interior design can create safe spaces that foster tranquility, connection, and longevity, and give ideas (big and small) for how to implement that. After all, this concept is not just for homeowners with lots of room—it is equally applicable to urban apartment dwellers or even folks living in dorms. Whether your space is long term or temporary, it is impactful to have it work for you where you are living *right now*.

We will discuss how to turn your home into a refuge that promotes health, happiness, and growth. From incorporating indoor greenery to installing soothing water features and embracing earthy textures, you will feel empowered to cultivate environments that evoke calm, contemplative design that allows for thoughtful living.

Biophilic design invokes multiple senses at once for an immersive, whole-body experience. In this space, the organic colors and combination of textures prompt the body's reaction to sight and touch, while the open window lets in fresh air that ignites our sense of smell.

Biophilic Basics

Before jumping into my method, I should first explain the principles of biophilic design. Stephen R. Kellert is a Yale professor, author, and preeminent expert on biophilia. He explains that biophilic design can be organized under three central pillars:

1. Incorporation of nature
2. Inspiration from nature
3. Interaction with nature

Incorporating nature in your home (through additions like plants and lighting) allows you to experience it directly and immediately benefit. So often, we move in and out of our homes and fall into an auto-response mode, forgetting to be present. Having these physical cues reminds us to stay grounded and live in the moment.

We may also gather **inspiration from nature** in a less direct way (say, through materials, motifs, colors, and shapes that remind us of things in nature). From a practical design perspective, we don't always have the luxury of living alongside a wide-open meadow or expansive ocean view, but we can use interior design to evoke a specific feeling nature gives us. Certain natural materials like wood or brick may even stimulate an emotional response if connected to a memory or feeling of comfort (a fond memory of a family log cabin, for example). We can harness those feelings in our current space by incorporating similar materials.

My dad has a master's degree in landscape architecture, and he taught me how important **interaction with nature** is to a person's mindset. I'd watch him design buildings and plan for landscaping that matched the style and purpose of each structure. I came to appreciate how outdoor elements aren't just decorative, they're essential to how we experience and move through a space. Dad was particularly passionate about pathways and flow, concepts that are integral to biophilic design. As we bring nature into our homes, it's equally important to consider how the natural world outside our window interacts with our spaces.

Biophilic design goes beyond decorating with plants. Here, handcraft meets nature in the home with crocheted monstera leaves that this homeowner created.

JENNY JACKSON
PINEAPPLE STREET
EMILY GIFFIN
MEANT TO BE

Consider the view beyond the walls when decorating. Everything from an inspiring vista to a greenery-covered wall can impact the feel of your interiors.

This includes sightlines to trees, thoughtfully placed garden beds, or seamless connections between indoors and out, all of which can transform a home into a place of harmony and renewal.

Kellert's research reveals that biophilic design doesn't just make spaces look beautiful—it transforms how we think, feel, and behave. Physically, it can lower blood pressure and reduce stress. Mentally, it helps us focus and feel more grounded in our day-to-day lives. Behaviorally, it sparks creativity and enhances problem-solving skills. But the impact goes even deeper. As Kellert beautifully sums it up: "This sense of positive relationship to nature ultimately motivates us to become good stewards and sustain these places over time."

The term "biophilia" was coined in the 1960s but didn't garner major attention until the '80s. Before then, modern architecture had evolved into something routinely lifeless and cookie cutter, so this concept helped bring the focus back to nature and its influence on living spaces.

Dissecting the term, you get "bio-," which means life or living things, and "-philia," which means love. Biophilia is literally the love of living things. And biophilic design incorporates that appreciation into a space's function and appearance.

Understanding the background of a new concept is important, but it's even easier to digest when you learn how to implement it into your own life. That's what this book will do: show you how to incorporate these concepts into your home design through accessible ideas that maximize the biophilic benefits and increase your love for your surroundings.

Throughout these pages, I've collected examples of biophilic design from my own projects and projects by other designers and photographers whose work I admire. Plus, I'll suggest specific techniques you can try as you kick-start your own biophilic makeover.

Some of these techniques may be more introspective while others will be more directly related to design. Let's start with how to feel grounded in your mind, which will help you feel grounded in other areas of your life. Rather than getting caught up in the shoulds, woulds, and coulds of the past or future-tripping about what might happen tomorrow, grounding techniques bring you back to the present moment. All of this requires active internal work. As with therapy, when we do our inner work, our external behavior adjusts.

Use artwork, materials, and textures to engage your senses and keep you feeling grounded in a space.

Get Grounded

TRY THIS MINDFULNESS TECHNIQUE

Pick a comfortable spot as your mindfulness corner where there is a plant, artwork, or some other visual cue to remind you about the intention of the space. When we pair a habit with a specific environment, the brain will start to connect the two.

One of my favorite mindfulness techniques doesn't require any tools other than utilizing your five senses. It's a simple way to clear your mind and guide yourself back to the present moment. Let's count down from five:

5. Name **five** things you can see.

4. Name **four** things you feel. This could either be an emotion or something you can physically feel (like, "I am feeling anxious" or "I am feeling this ceramic mug in my hands").

3. Identify **three** sounds that you can hear, and notice how loud or quiet they are.

2. Tell me **two** things that you can smell.

1. Finally, describe **one** thing you can taste.

How did this exercise change your awareness of your surroundings? Did you notice anything new or surprising during this process? What sense was easiest for you to focus on? Which was the most challenging? Consider if there was a particular sense that helped you feel most present and how you could incorporate that into your daily life more often.

WONDERPLANTS
Ellsworth Kelly Postcards

Nature by Design

Nature ignites our senses. It's not only about the things we see when we look around outdoors, but what we smell, hear, feel, and taste. I grew up in the Pacific Northwest, so being outdoors was a huge part of my life. We were always by the water or in the mountains, and my parents used that as inspiration in the interiors of the homes we lived in, typically using rich green and blue shades that evoked a sense of peace as well as place. These days, I'm a California girl, and the ocean plays a huge role in the design choices I make. No matter what your preference is when it comes to design, the key to biophilia is to use nature in a way that calms you rather than overstimulates you. You want to arouse your senses, not overpower them.

If you read my first book, *Home Therapy,* you'll notice biophilic elements implemented throughout many of the spaces (plants, woven textures, organic lines). That's because these features provide a natural way to infuse a sense of well-being and creativity into a physical environment. With *Grounded Living,* we'll dive deeper into maximizing nature's calming effects so that you can infuse your home with a sense of peace that will naturally bleed into other aspects of your life. First, let's start with some introspection.

Your inspiration from the great outdoors can be infused into your design without feeling overly kitschy. The headboard in this ocean-inspired bedroom mimics the movement of the water over rocks and seashells, while the bedside lamp is reminiscent of coral and the pendant of an anemone.

Identify Your Goals

Every space within your home has a purpose, but are you using that purpose to its fullest potential? The design of a room isn't just about how it looks; it's about its mood and function: how it makes you feel and what it empowers you to do. Corporations have embraced biophilic design for its power to fuel creativity, productivity, and collaboration—so why not harness that same power at home? Whether you want to spark your imagination, foster connection among housemates, provide a safe learning environment for your growing toddler, or simply create a haven for rest, your goals should guide every design choice.

Bring the comforts of the indoors to your outdoor space to enhance the experience and encourage you to linger longer and soak up the benefits of nature.

Ocean

Meadow

Desert

Mountain

Choose Your Biophilic Blueprint

As we move throughout this book, we'll refer to your "Biophilic Blueprint"—the natural setting that you find most peaceful, inspiring, and life-giving. This will be a compass to help you determine the direction to take your home design as you incorporate biophilic elements throughout your living space. You can change the blueprint at any time, but this reference point will help guide you along the way.

Close your eyes. Now picture yourself in nature anywhere in the world. Ask yourself the following questions:

Where did you end up? Are your toes digging into the warm sand by the sea or laced up in hiking boots on a winding mountain trail?

What do you smell? The earthy aroma of wet dewy grass? The crisp scent of pine needles in the forest? Or the sunbaked spice of dry desert air?

What time of day is it? Is the golden glow of sunrise just peeking over the horizon? Or is it the soft, muted light of twilight?

What is the season? Do you feel the coolness of autumn leaves beneath your feet? The warmth of the summer sun on your skin? Or the brisk chill of a winter breeze?

After noting your answers, choose from **ocean, meadow, desert,** or **mountain** based on your emotional connection and design preferences. Of course, these four environments are not the only options, but they provide a good starting point for most settings in nature.

Are you drawn to the wispy flowers of a meadow or the rustic woods of the mountains? Let your preferences guide your design choices.

Curate Your Space

Once you've identified your Biophilic Blueprint on the previous page, you'll want to identify nature-driven elements from it that you can incorporate into your home immediately. Think about adding a textural rug, rearranging furniture for better lounging, or bringing in a houseplant. Now, what are longer-term changes you can make to further enhance that vibe? Changing the wall color? Incorporating tile or replacing countertop materials? Swapping out light fixtures?

Within this step, you should also consider what season or time of day you are most drawn to. Decide if your inspiration is rooted in spring renewal, summer vibrancy, fall coziness, or winter tranquility. If it's spring, that will influence your color palette toward lighter and brighter shades than if you were to choose winter (which would suggest richer hues and heavier, cozy elements).

First, look at the four mood boards on the following spread. Is there one you gravitate toward most? Next, use the grid that follows to home in on the season within your Biophilic Blueprint that speaks to you most. Each box in the grid includes suggestions for **materials, textures, colors,** and **design elements** relevant to the season and Biophilic Blueprint of your choosing.

Botanical motifs provide an instant hit of nature. Look for wallpaper, artwork, and textiles that infuse your Biophilic Blueprint.

Incorporate suggested **materials** into furniture, decor, or even wall treatments.

Bring in **texture** or a tactile element that creates a sensory connection to nature.

Use the **color** palette examples as a guide for paint, fabric, and accessory choices.

Integrate specific **design elements** (like plants, art, and furniture) to enhance your chosen biophilic theme.

ORTIGIA

Ocean

Meadow

Desert

Mountain

	Ocean	Meadow
Spring	**Materials:** Driftwood, sea glass, linen **Textures:** Smooth, flowing, breezy fabrics **Colors:** Soft blues, whites, seafoam green, apricot **Design elements:** Wave-patterned decor, mirrors to reflect light, translucent curtains	**Materials:** Natural organic cotton, wildflower prints **Textures:** Soft, delicate fabrics **Colors:** Soft butter yellows, pastel pinks and greens, lilac **Design elements:** Floral artwork, sheer curtains, lace table runner
Summer	**Materials:** Rattan, woven seagrass **Textures:** Organic cotton and flax linens, woven shades, raffia **Colors:** Aqua blues, sandy neutrals, sun-bleached whites, coral pinks **Design elements:** Artifact shell displays, woven hammocks, seashell wind chime	**Materials:** Bamboo, natural fibers **Textures:** Soft, plush structure **Colors:** Bright greens, sunlit yellow, vibrant florals, soft peaches, sky blues **Design elements:** Grassland patterns, woven baskets, wildflower arrangements, picnic-inspired decor
Fall	**Materials:** Weathered metal, dark-stained wood, rope **Textures:** Knotted weaves, coarse woven fabrics **Colors:** Stormy blues, deep browns, navy, silver accents **Design elements:** Fringed throw blankets, pebble-textured rugs, distressed leather chairs	**Materials:** Hemp, dried florals **Textures:** Jute, burlap **Colors:** Muted marigold, olive green, deep umber, burnt sienna **Design elements:** Rustic wreath, wool throws, artisanal ceramic jugs, layered rugs, vintage brass objects
Winter	**Materials:** Frosted glass, shimmery metallics **Textures:** Plush velvets, faux fur, chunky knits **Colors:** Icy whites, pale blues, deep indigo, frosted blue-green **Design elements:** Nautical sculptures, reflective surfaces, frosted glass vases, white coral decor	**Materials:** Wicker, wool **Textures:** Cozy weaves, natural stone, stained wood, unlacquered brass **Colors:** Evergreen, snowy whites, plum, fir green, moody burgundy **Design elements:** Wreaths made from dried flowers, vintage mismatched chairs, pattern-on-pattern upholstery

Desert

Materials: Light-toned wood (oak and birch), smooth ceramics, linen

Textures: Airy and breathable natural fibers

Colors: Warm tans, soft peaches, dusty greens, muted coral, sandy taupe

Design elements: Minimalist wooden furniture with curved edges, handmade pottery in earth tones, woven baskets

Materials: Bamboo, natural stone, cotton textiles

Textures: Crisp and airy fabrics

Colors: Sun-warmed ochre, burnt orange, terra-cotta red, soft ivory

Design elements: Low-profile furniture, boho-style cotton throws and pillows, Moroccan kilim rugs

Materials: Dark-stained wood, matte ceramics, wool blends

Textures: Layered, cozy, and rich elements

Colors: Deep mahogany, rust orange, sandstone, warm grays

Design elements: Minimalist wooden shelving, black ceramic for contrast, handcrafted details

Materials: Heavy wool, raw stone, brass, shou sugi ban (charred wood)

Textures: Rough, tactile elements

Colors: Deep gold, smoky gray, metallic bronze, rich browns

Design elements: Desert-inspired ceramics in moody palettes, subtle geometric patterns, sculptural desert plants

Mountain

Materials: Reclaimed wood, natural stone, linen

Textures: Rugged and layered feel with soft natural fibers

Colors: Earthy browns, mossy green, cool gray, slate blue

Design elements: Stone sculptures, cozy knits, rustic wooden accents, antique brass, potted ferns

Materials: Pine wood, wool, wicker

Textures: Thick and cozy with breathable fabrics

Colors: Deep forest green, midnight blue, earthy red, weathered brown

Design elements: Cabin-inspired decor, lantern lighting, vintage botanical prints, open shelving

Materials: Cedarwood, faux fur, heavy wool

Textures: Warm layers, cable knits, wool blends

Colors: Muted grays, rich auburn, burnt sienna, golden amber

Design elements: Fireplace mantel, plaid patterns, pine scents, leather-bound books

Materials: Stone, heavy wool, suede, dark-stained wood

Textures: Rugged and natural pieces with plush and cozy accents

Colors: Charcoal gray, snowy white

Design elements: Log cabin inspiration, faux fur throws, checkered upholstery or drapery

THOMAS PROCTOR
CLASSICAL HOUSES
A TALE OF INTERIORS
PIERCE & WARD

Sustainability Spotlight

Appreciation Inspires Action

Growing up surrounded by lush forests, crisp air, and a community that valued recycling and upcycling, I learned early on that our connection to nature shapes how we care for it. Volunteering with environmentally focused organizations as a teen and young adult instilled in me a profound respect for the environment. To this day, my mom still chides me if I mix up compost, recycling, and regular trash. These roots of sustainability—living authentically and mindfully—have become the foundation of my personal values and design philosophy.

As a designer, I've grown acutely aware of the materials and choices I bring into my clients' homes. Sustainability isn't just about aesthetics; it's about creating spaces that support well-being without compromising the planet or our health. Whether it's selecting paints labeled "low VOC" (volatile organic compounds) for a family sensitive to allergens or with young children, incorporating natural light for a client struggling with seasonal affective disorder, or choosing durable, responsibly sourced furniture, every decision is an opportunity to align our values with the way we live.

Biophilic design amplifies this connection. By bringing nature into our homes—whether through greenery, natural light, or materials that reflect the earth—we're reminded of its beauty and importance. And when we live surrounded by elements of nature, we're inspired to protect it. The simple act of appreciating the natural world in our spaces can foster a deep desire to preserve it for generations to come.

This isn't just a design choice; it's a mindset. Sustainability starts with awareness and intention, and biophilia bridges the gap between loving nature and living in harmony with it. This is why biophilic design isn't just about creating beautiful homes—it's about creating a ripple effect of care, mindfulness, and stewardship for the world around us.

When creating a room, try to focus on sustainable options, like low VOC paint, natural materials (like rattan, shown here), a thrifted coffee table, and an heirloom sofa.

There are no hard-and-fast rules to follow in biophilic design. It's simply a method of incorporating natural elements, motifs, shapes, sounds, and smells into your environment to make you feel more at ease.

Whether you're seeking refuge from the stresses of daily life, interested in cultivating a deeper connection with the natural world, or wanting to foster a sense of peace and security in a chaotic time, your home should nourish your whole self. Let's use biophilic design to unlock the transformative potential of your living space. We'll start with perhaps the most obvious: inviting nature inside.

Living rooms and bedrooms aren't the only spaces for biophilic design. A dining room can provide a great opportunity to use nature to ignite conversation and invite connection.

Bringing the Outdoors In

As a therapist making house calls, I walked into countless homes that were cluttered with the complexities of life and quickly learned that a space can either amplify stress or become a powerful tool for healing. On these visits, I began to introduce simple biophilic elements—a potted fern in the entryway, a vase of fresh flowers on the kitchen table, or even sheer curtains to invite more sunlight into the living room. The changes were small but profound and reinvigorated not just the space, but the emotional energy of the home. When I look back at my own design evolution (from my graduate school apartment to my current house), I realize that nature has always played a part in making me feel good at home. Organic colors, natural textures, and a bounty of plants all bring elements of the outdoor environment inside our living spaces. Incorporating greenery indoors has had proven positive effects for decades. Just think about the sense of calm you feel when your home is infused with the scent of freshly cut flowers. Natural elements like this help improve mental clarity, memory, and productivity. Their presence helps lower blood pressure and reduce the cognitive load. So as a therapist, I sincerely believe that adding nature and nature-inspired motifs throughout your decor has the power to influence your thoughts, emotions, and behaviors. And as an interior designer, I recognize the effects these elements have on people's experiences within a space—most important, the experience in our own home. Plants, natural materials and motifs, and organic colors can be used to kick-start the benefits of biophilia throughout your interior.

Why let a home workout space feel utilitarian? Here, bold wallpaper and decorative sconces add visual interest that detract from the machinery and a wood slat wall provides separation without making you feel completely boxed in. Plus, potted plants enhance the quality of the air.

Ease into Green

Whether you're starting with a blank slate or you want to add natural elements to your existing decor, there are plenty of ways to make biophilia work for you.

Conceivably the easiest or most straightforward place to start is by introducing plants. Place a potted plant in the bathroom, your home office, or the entryway, and you'll notice an almost instant grounding feeling. Plants have roots, right? Well, their presence has the ability to root us in a space by keeping us in the moment. You don't need to have a green thumb to feel at home with plants, either. Faux plants will give your brain the same positive reaction as real ones without the stress of pruning and maintenance.

I did a podcast with plant expert Darryl Cheng a while back and he gave me this incredible "aha" moment about nature: When I would care for plants, I'd take browning leaves so seriously and so personally. But Darryl reminded me that they're simply part of the circle of life; they make room for new growth. That paradigm shift—embracing how nature course-corrects itself—was eye-opening.

Embrace Imperfection

Darryl also showed me the beauty of flexibility in caring for plants: There's no judgment, no need to take things personally, just a natural rhythm to follow. Consider this same analogy for your home: Your space will evolve. The spark that certain elements once ignited for you may fizzle out. But rather than feeling guilty about that, remove them to make space for new inspiration to enter.

In all things, I always want to encourage people to embrace imperfection rather than view it as some kind of failure. Living imperfectly is what makes us authentic beings. I call myself a "reformed perfectionist" and every day I continue to make progress toward accepting a more go-with-the-flow mentality. Years ago, I received a hand-me-down Amish coffee table from a neighbor. She told me it was perfect for little kids because all the banging and wear would only add to its character. I accepted it with such relief—the table was beautiful, yes, but I also didn't have to worry about it fitting into my lifestyle with young children.

There's a mantra I often repeat to myself and my clients:

> *My home nurtures my well-being and tells my story. I will focus on what feels good for me, trusting that it's exactly as it's meant to be.*

Understanding the difference between what is in your control and what is not can be a freeing feeling.

Pay attention to the details in your design. Whether you pair plants or art with floral wallpaper or find a unique piece of furniture that mimics natural curves or crevices found in nature, it is intention that will make your space distinctive.

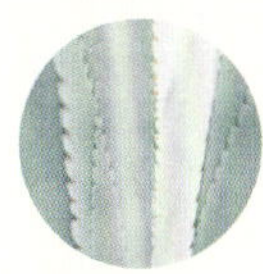

Be Intentional

With every new item you bring into your home, consider the meaning behind it. What does this amber vase remind you of? What feeling does this rough-hewn console table give you? When each element holds a personal connection, your space becomes more than just a collection of objects—it's a reflection of your story. Feeling connected to your space makes you want to linger in it, to care for it, and, in turn, to let it care for you.

Before bringing something new into your home, ask yourself: *What job will this item have in my space?* Maybe it's there to inspire you, like a framed quote that reminds you of your goals. Perhaps it's meant to ground you, like a cozy chair in a reading nook that invites you to slow down. Or maybe it serves as a productivity boost, like a well-placed desk lamp that keeps you focused. When every piece has a purpose—whether practical, emotional, or aspirational—your space becomes an intentional reflection of your life and values.

Nature's Cue

The Power of Scent

We all digest information from the world around us in different ways. There are visual learners who experience through sight, auditory learners who pick up on what they hear, and kinesthetic learners who absorb best through doing or touching. I believe that a person can respond to nature in different ways, too, but that we all have penchants for one particular experience.

As someone who struggles with anxiety, I have learned how powerful scents can be in shaping my mood and grounding my thoughts. The neurotransmitters in our olfactory system spark our body's response to stimuli, making aromatherapy a simple yet impactful tool. Consider introducing scents to amplify that sense in your environment through the incorporation of candles, room sprays, or dried flowers. You could even simply open a window and let the fresh air flow through your space to refresh your mood.

opposite: Hang dried eucalyptus from your shower head for an invigorating scent. Those with allergies can breathe easy and replace the eucalyptus with banana leaves to get the botanical benefits without any sneeze-inducing smells.

above: Candles, potpourri, and diffusers are small investments that offer huge benefits.

Bringing the outdoors in doesn't just mean incorporating plants within your decor. You should also consider colors and textures that evoke a feeling of the natural world.

CHANEL

Biophilic Paint

Instantly conjure the effects of the great outdoors through color. Here are just a few examples from each of the four main Biophilic Blueprints to give you a quick visual.

Ocean

Meadow

Desert

Mountain

Naturally Textured

Additionally, incorporating fibers and finishes found outdoors throughout your interior space will influence the overall effect of bringing nature indoors.

Jute, Sisal, and Hemp
Natural-fiber rugs and textiles add warmth and durability.

Wood Textures
Varied finishes, from raw, reclaimed wood to polished hardwood, add a tactile, earthy feel.

Bamboo
Lightweight and sustainable, this material can be used for blinds, flooring, and even bedding.

Cork
Opt for flooring, wall panels, or decor that maximizes cork's natural beauty and sound-dampening properties.

Leather and Hide
This material brings in warmth and a grounding texture in rugs, upholstery, or accents. For a more sustainable option, shop vintage (vegan leathers may be cruelty-free but are made from plastic).

Wool and Linen
Natural fabrics add softness, insulation, and a cozy feel.

Organic Cotton and Muslin
Light, airy fabrics are perfect for drapery and bedding.

Clay and Terra-cotta
Choose vases, tiles, or trinkets that provide a warm, handmade quality.

Stone
Granite, marble, or other natural stones typically feature organic movement in their patterns.

Sand
Rough, gritty textures or even fabrics that incorporate the light shade of sand evoke the natural world.

Unique Wall Treatments
Venetian plaster, limewash, and other surface treatments can help infuse a typically man-made material with an organic quality.

Maximize the function of every corner and add some biophilic flair while you're at it. Here, a soft, channeled banquet offers soothing texture and anchors the space, while greenery in a large terracotta planter balances out the scale.

A custom green velvet headboard (easily DIY-ed) stretches across the back wall and feels like moss on the forest floor.

Force of Habit

I have always been drawn to cognitive behavioral therapy (CBT). CBT is a common method of mental health treatment that acknowledges that our thoughts influence our emotions, and our emotions influence our behaviors. When we get positive reinforcement about some kind of action, we want to repeat that to continue the good feeling. The goal is to ultimately form good habits that help us feel better in our home so that we can feel calmer, more productive, and organized. To me, biophilia is a subtle form of CBT. Representations of nature throughout my living space serve as gentle reminders of the beauty in the world around me and help me to stay present.

CBT also highlights the importance of self-soothing for stress relief. In the middle of a recent sleepless night, I caught the soft glow of moonlight on the leaves of my fiddle-leaf fig. Its quiet presence felt steadying, like a gentle nudge back to calm. Identifying this natural beauty in my surroundings helped activate the relaxed feeling that actually being in nature gives me. Therefore, we can link motifs to get an emotional reset as well.

Note how the smooth stone coffee table is offset by the natural fiber rug. This balance of tactile elements makes a space feel luxuriously layered.

Get Grounded

LIVEN UP A SHELF

Shelves aren't just for storing—they're for storytelling. They offer a chance to showcase the harmony between nature and each person's unique journey. When styling, I start with nature's four elements:

earth, like wood, crystal, stone, or greenery;

fire, with candles or a small light source;

water, through reflective metallics or shimmery accents; and, of course,

air, the most essential element of all. Breathing room between vignettes allows qi (or energy) to flow and gives each grouping its own platform to shine.

Include at least three items from these categories and mix them among your favorite photos, books, and mementos to bring energy and life into your space.

opposite: Your initial instinct might be to pair a green or beige sofa with this leafy green wallpaper, but the unexpected blue upholstery adds just the right amount of contrast to the space (similar to the view of a dense tree canopy against the sky above).

below: Zellige tile has a pearlescent quality that will instantly transport you to the seaside.

FRANZEN
THE ESSEX SERPENT
KEROUAC ON THE ROAD
MORE THAN JUST A HOUSE
BASQUIAT
DAVID CHANG
MIKE NICHOLS
Mel Brooks All About Me!
IN THE COMPANY OF WOMEN

Bountiful branches and well-presented produce add life and a breath of fresh air to this spacious kitchen.

Nature's Cue
No Boundaries

Indoor plants aren't just for corners and tabletops—they can thrive in surprising places throughout your home, adding a touch of nature's beauty wherever you choose to place them. Transform your bathroom into a tropical retreat by suspending cascading vines like spider plants or philodendron from the shower rod (or ceiling!). Their low-light, lush foliage will love the humidity and turn your bathing routine into an even more soothing experience.

For a bold statement, turn an unused staircase landing into a vertical garden oasis. Install floating shelves and arrange a mix of air-purifying greenery like snake plants, rubber plants, or dracaena, creating living artwork that greets you as you ascend.

Ultimately, aim to discover the untapped possibilities in your space. Hang plants above doorways or let a trailing variety cascade down the railing of your staircase. A sturdy bookshelf can easily double as a garden bed, holding smaller pots of herbs or succulents in the heart of your living area. Use unique planters like vintage teacups, driftwood logs, or even recycled glass candle jars to infuse your greenery with personality and make it feel like an integral part of your home's vibe.

top: Turn an awkward nook into a lush oasis.

bottom: Go ahead, let your plants grow wild! They'll provide drama at the right scale for a large room.

opposite: Humidity-loving plants will thrive in a bathroom. Reserve some counter space for a favorite pot or install floating shelves to keep them on display.

Anita's Plant Picks

When it comes to bringing life into a space, I always find myself coming back to these tried-and-true plants. They're not just pretty to look at—they actually *do* something for your home. Whether it's adding a touch of calm, purifying the air, or simply making a room feel more inviting, these green beauties earn their keep. They're my go-to plants for adding a natural design element that makes a space feel layered, intentional, and alive. If you're looking for plants that are both stylish and low maintenance, these are my favorites.

Beginner-Friendly Plants

Satin Pothos

This trailing beauty combines easy care with stunning aesthetics. Its velvety, silver-speckled leaves look luxurious draped over a shelf or cascading from a hanging planter. Satin pothos tolerates low light and occasional missed waterings, making it a stress-free way to add texture and movement to your space. Think of it as the jewelry that completes your room's outfit—effortless and elegant.

Moonshine Snake Plant

With its striking, silver-green upright leaves, the moonshine snake plant is modern minimalism in plant form. It's nearly indestructible and thrives in low light, dry air, and with irregular care. It's also a nighttime oxygen booster, making it ideal for a bedroom. If you're the kind of person who wants their home to look polished with minimal effort, this plant is your perfect match.

Air-Purifying Plants

Stromanthe Triostar

This plant is a showstopper with its vibrant pink, green, and cream leaves—like a living piece of art. Beyond its striking appearance, the stromanthe triostar works quietly to purify the air in your home. It thrives in bright, indirect light and loves a bit of humidity, making it an ideal choice for bathrooms or kitchens.

Rubber Plant

With its creamy variegated leaves and striking upright form, the rubber plant is a bold yet elegant statement for any room. This plant doesn't just elevate your decor—it actively works to purify the air, making it a smart and stylish choice for your living room or office. Give it a spot with bright, indirect light, and watch it thrive as the centerpiece of your space.

The Clean Air Collective

For those who want a healthier home, the "clean air collective" combines plants known for their air-purifying superpowers. A classic trio like the **areca palm, peace lily,** and **rubber plant** works overtime to filter toxins and freshen up your space. Perfect for bedrooms or living areas, these plants bring style and science into your sanctuary.

Lucky Leaf Duo

This pair is all about abundance, luck, and positive energy. The **Chinese money plant,** with its round, coin-like leaves, symbolizes wealth and connection, while **lucky bamboo** is believed to attract prosperity and harmony. Together, they make the perfect combo for your home office, entryway, or anywhere you want to invite success and good fortune. Plus, they're both easy to care for—so you can ensure that luck won't run out!

Trailing Plants

Combined Ivy (Classic + Trailing)

Ivy is a timeless favorite for its graceful, cascading vines and ability to thrive almost anywhere. Whether it's the classic variety or a more dramatic trailing type, ivy adds softness and movement to any space. Let it spill over a bookshelf, hang it in a planter, or drape it around a window.

String of Hearts

Delicate and romantic, string of hearts is a trailing plant with thin, heart-shaped leaves in shades of green and purple. Its long, slender vines are perfect for creating a whimsical, dreamy vibe. This plant thrives in bright, indirect light and grows quickly, adding beauty to any home.

String of Nickels

This charming trailing plant is named for its round, coin-like leaves that bring a soft, cascading elegance to your home. Its lush vines create a layered, organic look that beautifully offsets other natural textures like wood or stone. Thriving in bright, indirect light with a touch of humidity, it's an ideal choice for kitchens and bathrooms.

Hoya Carnosa Tricolor

This vibrant trailing plant is a showstopper with its mix of green, white, and pink leaves. The Hoya carnosa tricolor brings a playful pop of color to your home while requiring little care in return. It thrives in bright, indirect light and rewards your patience with delicate star-shaped flowers, making it a true gem for plant enthusiasts.

Feel-Good Greenery

Jade Plant

The jade plant is a symbol of good fortune and prosperity in Chinese culture, and is often gifted as a housewarming plant in many cultures. Its thick, rounded leaves are said to resemble coins, making it a favorite for bringing financial luck. Place it near the entrance of your home or in a sunny window to invite positivity and growth.

Peperomia Green

With its thick, glossy leaves and compact size, Peperomia green would be a cheerful addition. This versatile plant thrives in medium to bright, indirect light and adapts well to small spaces like shelves, desks, or windowsills. It's a wonderful choice for bringing a pop of greenery to your home with minimal fuss—proof that good things come in small packages.

list continues →

Shady Partners

Meet the ultimate low-light tag team: the **snake plant** and **zz plant.** These resilient beauties thrive in the dimmest corners of your home, offering a sleek blend of upright, architectural leaves and rich green foliage. Whether they're tucked into a shadowy hallway or livening up a bathroom, these shady partners prove that you don't need sunlight to create a vibrant, grounded space.

Boston Fern

The Boston fern is a lush and vibrant plant that symbolizes growth and renewal. Its cascading fronds add softness and movement while also improving air quality. Known for its ability to thrive in humid conditions, it's a wonderful choice for bathrooms, kitchens, or any room where you want to create a calming, spa-like atmosphere.

Statement Plants for Design

Monstera

The monstera earns the nickname "cheese plant" with its iconic split leaves that look like they've been delicately hand-cut. This plant grows quickly and makes an instant design statement, whether you're styling a cozy corner or filling an empty wall space with greenery. Perfect for larger rooms, the monstera thrives in bright, indirect light and grows with a wild, sculptural elegance that never goes out of style.

Maidenhair Fern

Soft and delicate, the maidenhair fern brings a touch of whimsy to your home. Its fine, lacelike leaves and gentle cascading form make it a beautiful addition to any space crying out for softness and movement. Though it prefers higher humidity and consistent watering, its graceful beauty makes the extra care worth it. Display it on a side table or a windowsill for a dreamy, natural vibe.

Olive Tree

Olive trees bring a timeless Mediterranean elegance to any space, and I love their silvery-green leaves and sculptural quality. While they're typically better suited for outdoor environments, they can thrive indoors with the right care. To keep an olive tree happy inside, ensure it gets plenty of sunlight—at least six hours a day—and maintain a warm, dry environment. If these conditions aren't realistic, a high-quality artificial olive tree can offer the same aesthetic appeal with less maintenance.

The Perfect Pair

Some plants just belong together. Pair bold, upright greenery like a **rubber plant** or **snake plant** with something softer, like **trailing ivy** or a **maidenhair fern,** to create balance and visual interest. This combination works beautifully in entryways, living rooms, or any space where you want a mix of texture and height. It's an easy way to let your plants complement each other—and your home.

The potted tree in this room is faux for easy upkeep, but styling an arrangement of fresh flowers nearby helps trick the eye (and our mood) into thinking it's all real.

Home
KINFOLK

Get Grounded

USE NATURE TO INSPIRE CREATIVITY

Have you noticed how being in an uninspiring space can leave you feeling bored and unmotivated? But have you ever felt this way in your favorite natural hangout (on a sandy beach or hiking a mountain trail)? Likely not. That's because when our surroundings are aesthetically pleasing, our curiosity and creativity peak. Harness this within your home by sparking creativity in workspaces like the home office or kitchen by using natural elements.

Let your home be your creative playground because the more you can play and be yourself, the more authentic you can truly become. Having a creative outlet can reduce stress, limit anxiety, and prevent burnout. You don't have to be good at the hobby you choose, but if it fires you up and breaks you out of your typical routine, it can increase self-confidence.

left: Keep crafting supplies tucked away but easily within reach for whenever you feel the creative itch.

right: Here, botanical wallpaper, layers of potted plants, and an infusion of natural textures (like rattan chairs and visible wood grain on the beams) provides a motivating backdrop to a combo home office and craft space.

Strength in numbers: A grouping of woven pendant lights, a pair of rattan swings, and layers of linen curtains give this exterior hangout a luxe indoor vibe that enhances the porch's outdoor view.

A SWEET FLORAL LIFE

Use Figurative Inspiration

When leaning on a particular landscape as your design influence, you might worry that the space could start to feel kitschy or theme-y. That's where the biophilic concept of "inspiration from nature" really comes into play. While bringing the outdoors in literally through plants and other natural elements is key, incorporating figurative inspiration is equally as important. In nature, we see fractals (complex geometric patterns) in shells, tree branches, and snowflakes, so consider how you could incorporate those types of patterns into your designs.

Take this ocean-inspired lounge space (opposite). Nothing in it really screams "OCEAN" at you, but upon closer inspection, you'll find tons of nautical inspiration. The dusty-blue moiré wallpaper, the clamshell-inspired mirror, the ripple effect on the console doors, and even the curves of much of the furniture give off a sense of the surf.

In nature, we rarely see a bounty of perfect right angles, but typically more curves and spirals. The natural geometry of these elements should influence motifs and finishes used throughout our interiors. Plus, our brain's visual cortex identifies these curves as safer than more aggressive sharp angles and encourages relaxation (as opposed to stimulating vigilance).

opposite: Nothing is overly nautical in this surf-inspired space, but the inspiration is still apparent. The gallery wall is arranged organically with a few pieces of landscape artwork that give off a bird's-eye view of the coast.

Channel Nature's Patterns

These days, many popular design styles home in on comfort—and biophilic design is no exception. Rather than striving for rigid perfection, let's celebrate life's eccentricities. In nature, we are often captivated by imperfection and asymmetry (just think of the coil of a snail shell or the leaning limbs of a tree).

In Japanese tradition, appreciation of imperfection is known as "wabi sabi." An example of wabi sabi in action is the Japanese art of kintsugi, which is the method of mending cracked or broken ceramics with gold leaf. Instead of hiding the cracks, the metal highlights them and shows off the item's transformation into something beautiful.

The Japanese also have a floral design style known as ikebana, which is meditative and often produces an asymmetrical result. Ikebana follows the organic lines of the stems being used in each arrangement.

Similarly, asymmetry in design tends to draw us in. That deliberate imbalance prompts our brain to analyze or engage with it. This is referred to as visual tension and can be used to direct a person's experience of a room. When we intentionally place something off-balance, we guide a person's eyes to that spot as a starting point.

Pattern and repetition can be soothing, while off-kilter elements draw us in to take a closer look. Both work together to make a space satisfying and engaging. (I mean, just look at the woodwork leading to these stairs!)

THE VOGUE SEWING BOOK
SINGER

Nature's Cue
Animal Magnetism

Another easy way to bring nature into your interior space is by incorporating animal motifs—whether subtly or boldly. A simple glass bird perched on a shelf, framed wildlife photos from your travels, or wallpaper featuring a favorite species can instantly transport you to the natural world. For those who desire a more maximalist approach, layering textures and patterns inspired by the animal kingdom can create a lush, immersive experience. Plush faux-fur throws and animal-shaped pillows, richly patterned fabrics with jungle or forest scenes, or statement pieces like leopard-print ottomans and feathered accents can infuse a space with warmth and personality.

In our home, we love adding playful feline designs—even though one of my daughters is highly allergic to cats! From a charming ceramic cat pitcher to the adorable kitty-shaped planters in her room, it's our way of embracing our love for feline friends without the sneezing fits. Celebrate what you love in creative ways, layering elements that bring joy and connection to create a space that truly encompasses you.

Think past the animal hide when designing with animal motifs: Whether you're inspired by ocean creatures, backyard birds, or safari animals, you can find creative and kind ways of bringing these magnificent creatures home.

When possible, keep curtains wider than your windows to maximize sightlines.

If You've Got It, Flaunt It

If you are lucky enough to have a stunning outdoor view, magnify it! Make that window as large as possible. Position your fixtures and furniture in a way that strengthens sightlines to what Mother Nature has put on display or avoids covering them up. Go for an extra-long curtain rod so that your drapes can open all the way. Your view doesn't have to be a sprawling scene, either. It could be a lush wall of greenery and perennials or a trickle of a stream. Just consider this your reminder to look to what is literally sitting right outside your window as a potential design feature.

And If You Don't . . .

Every space may not offer the full package capped off with an idyllic outdoor scene, but we can surely find at least one positive. I mean, there's a reason you rented or bought the place, right? Maybe it's one window where the morning light streams in or a beautiful bathroom with a rain showerhead. I would dare to say that the one thing that initially drew you in is likely related to nature in some way because we are organic beings and that is naturally what entices us. Once you identify what that natural element is, build on that with other biophilic principles to maximize its benefits within your space.

And not all is lost if a nice view out the window isn't in the cards. Supplement with images of those desired scenes—photos and artwork have been proven to be similarly stimulating.

This bright white space still exudes tons of character and wild charm thanks to the bold zebra wallpaper tucked into the kitchen's breakfast nook.

wonderland

Get Some Air

Another (unseen) way to let the outdoors in? Fresh air! Whether through an open window or door, the infusion of fresh air can make a huge difference in how we feel. We spend 90 percent of our time indoors and the air quality there can be very poor. Stale indoor air can lead to headaches and fatigue, or even exacerbate respiratory issues, but a gentle breeze from outside can boost airflow, reduce indoor pollutants, and refresh your entire space. The magic lies in operable windows that allow cross-ventilation and air to move about freely.

Take advantage of good weather whenever you can and throw open doors and windows.

Woven Histories

Cut a Path

Just as animals create paths through the woods and rivers cut courses through rock, we can influence the flow around our interiors by highlighting pathways. It makes logical sense when animals do this. We once lived in an especially remote area. If you looked out to the left, you'd see the mountain and to the right was the lake. Like clockwork, we'd watch as the deer came down from the mountain to drink water at the lake. They chose a path of least resistance, and their daily trek made sense. Similarly in our homes, we should carve out these avenues from one area into the next that encourage whatever activity we want to happen there. Make an obvious walkway from the family room into the kitchen for kids to find snacks or facilitate flow from the informal entry of the home directly to the drop zone to avoid the dreaded pileup.

Plus, when a route through or out of a space is unclear, that can lead to feelings of anxiety. And if furniture is positioned too closely, you risk bumping your knee, which is frustrating. As natural beings, when we identify a clear pathway, we typically feel more secure.

Use rugs, lighting, and open space as a road map to lead people through each area and direct them where you want them to go.

WONDERLAND SUMMER
Climbing Rock
ADVENTURESS

Botanical prints and color choices combined with natural materials, like the ultra-organic coffee table, and topped off with fresh florals make for a homey, nature-inspired space.

Designing with Light

When it comes to biophilic design, I believe it's all about working with what the space gives you—embracing its natural flow, rather than fighting against it. However, there are some instances when you may need to be a bit more heavy-handed in your involvement. Take my house, for example. It has windows on only one side of each room, so light comes in one way: either in the morning or afternoon. Over time, I began to feel the effects of that lack of light on my mood. In fact, it was a real eye-opener when I learned that this was a form of depression known as seasonal affective disorder, or SAD.

When we finally decided to remodel after ten years of living in the house, I knew the first thing I wanted was a skylight in the bathroom. It might sound dramatic, but adding that skylight breathed new life into the space. The bathroom went from a spot I avoided to a personal sanctuary where I meditate, do yoga, and get ready for the day.

Now, I know not everyone is in a position to cut holes in their roof and add skylights (it took me a decade to get there, after all!), but that doesn't mean you can't work your magic with light in other ways. Simple tweaks like using reflective surfaces, selecting the right paint colors, and investing in thoughtfully chosen light bulbs can completely transform even a windowless room.

Knowing how to enhance or detract from the light in each space will make it that much more functional for your needs.

HOME THERAPY
BILL CUNNINGHAM

Light doesn't just brighten a space—it changes how we feel and function in it. Biophilic design takes this into account, using both natural and artificial light to create an environment that promotes well-being. Neuroscience proves that soft, diffused lighting calms the nervous system, helping us feel relaxed and at ease, while harsh lighting can make us feel on edge. And, of course, exposure to bright, natural light during the day is key for regulating our circadian rhythm and improving our sleep. So adding thoughtful lighting is a must in spaces that nurture comfort and balance.

Just as light is critical to life, it is a main element in biophilic design. The open ironwork on the stair rail allows light to pour into an otherwise dark dining space.

Reflect Light Creatively

When natural light is limited, my first instinct is to crave it, so I try to get resourceful with the ways I bounce light around. Sure, we can bring in lamps and utilize light bulbs to brighten things up, but my preference is to start by maximizing the natural structure of the space. Strategically hang mirrors opposite windows to create the illusion of more windows.

Additionally, incorporating reflective materials like acrylic, glass, and metal will continue to extend the light throughout your home. These pieces also help a room feel airier and less enclosed.

Illuminate from Above

Skylights and sun tunnels can have a major impact as well—in fact, the difference can feel like night and day. Allowing natural light to enter from the top down feels most balanced to me, as the whole room gets flooded with sunshine. While skylights may take more intense retrofitting work, sun tunnels are a relatively pain-free way to make a huge difference in a space. Also known as solar tubes, they draw sunlight from your roof through a flexible silver tube into any area that could use a brightness boost. Think dark hallways, closets, and anywhere you could use more light to be productive.

Shine On

Whether illuminating dark areas, accentuating tall ceilings, or making small spaces feel more expansive, skylights and sun tunnels have a major impact on the overall feeling of a home.

To me, skylights and sun tunnels are a cut above other light sources.

SHAMSHIRI
HUMANS
THE VOGUE SEWING BOOK

Play with Paint

Light reflective value (LRV) is a measurement of how much visible light a paint color reflects or absorbs, rated on a scale from 0 percent, which reflects no light (pure black), to 100 percent, which reflects all light (pure white). Every paint chip should have the LRV listed on the back for easy reference.

LRV is a factual element that can make choosing paint colors feel a little less daunting. When I select paint colors, I think about how my choices will best enhance the natural light in each space:

- If you have a darker room, opt for paint colors with higher percentages of LRV (70 percent and above) to make it feel brighter and more open.
- If you'd prefer the space to feel a little cozier, choose a mid-range LRV (around 40 to 60 percent).

Selecting the appropriate paint sheen is equally as helpful in brightening up a room. I like to use high-gloss paint strategically to help bounce light around. I recently painted a client's dining room in a mossy green shade and opted for the same shade on the ceiling in a high-gloss sheen that reflects both the natural light streaming in from the windows as well as the artificial light from the chandelier. It gives the illusion of a taller space as well!

Use lower gloss finishes (like flat or eggshell) when you want to create a moodier vibe or hope to minimize imperfections or texture on a wall. In rooms with lots of natural light, lower gloss finishes tone down the intensity, offering a more balanced, relaxed feel. The key is to think about how you want the light to behave—do you want it bright and airy, or warm and wrapped around you? The right sheen helps set the mood just as much as the color itself.

Redefine what colors you consider to be "neutral" and draw your inspiration from shades commonly found in nature.

Here, the color palette is inspired by the nearby Blue Ridge Mountains. The slate blue paint color doesn't feel too dark thanks to a plethora of windows and the mid-range LRV of the color choice.

Get Grounded

USE LRV TO AFFECT A ROOM'S MOOD

We can align our color choices with the natural cycles of the year to create a harmonious, nature-inspired home environment. Here, I've broken down four potential seasonal palettes.

Spring: In Full Bloom

Inspired by the rejuvenation of spring, this palette features fresh and airy tones that evoke growth, lightness, and new beginnings. Opt for soft pastels like pale yellow, mint green, sky blue, and warm beige with an LRV between 60 and 85 percent. These colors will reflect ample light, making spaces feel open, bright, and energizing. Plus, they mirror the vibrancy of new plant growth, evoking feelings of renewal and optimism.

Where to Use: Try these colors in bedrooms or nurseries to promote a sense of calm and vitality, aligning with circadian rhythms.

Summer: Golden Escape

Capture the vibrancy and warmth of summer with radiant and energizing tones that evoke sunlit beaches and warm horizons. Think turquoise, coral, light-to-medium blue greens, and warm sandy neutrals with an LRV between 50 and 70 percent. These shades balance brightness with depth, which is ideal for spaces where both energy and a touch of coziness are desired.

Where to Use: Living rooms and sunrooms would benefit from these colors, which evoke summer's vitality and enhance indoor-outdoor flow.

Fall: Slanted Light

Warm, grounded tones inspired by autumn's golden leaves and soft light create a cozy, comforting atmosphere. Consider burnt orange, yellow ochre, deep red, warm taupe, and shades of brown with an LRV of 30 to 50 percent. These earthy tones mimic the colors of falling leaves and natural transitions, fostering a sense of stability and reflection.

Where to Use: Use these in a dining room or library to create intimate, nurturing spaces.

Winter: Velvet Chill

Deep, moody tones that evoke the quiet elegance of winter are ideal for creating intimate, dramatic spaces. Navy blue, charcoal gray, forest green, and dark purple in a low LRV (between 10 and 30 percent) will absorb light, adding depth and richness to a space, while also maintaining a sense of tranquility. These shades mimic twilight skies and evergreen forests.

Where to Use: A primary bedroom or home office would benefit from these shades, as they promote focus and introspection. Used on furniture, these moody tones will help anchor a room. And when used on the ceiling, they could create a cocooning effect.

Window Dressing

As a decorative tactic, window coverings add lovely layers and encourage the eye to move upward within a room. But as far as function goes, consider the needs of the space and what type of window treatment would best accommodate those needs.

Sheer panels are a favorite of mine for secondary spaces because they offer some privacy while still allowing natural light to filter in. These are best used in areas like a secondary entrance where privacy is not the main focus.

Now, in my mother's new home, she has an entryway *full* of windows. Great in theory, until you feel like you're living in a fishbowl on display at night. For her, we opted for a textured window film that mimics reeded glass. Again, this allows the light to stream in but doesn't add any unnecessary bulk (or cost a fortune).

Floor-to-ceiling drapes add a dramatic grounding element along a wall of windows, while the light-filtering fabric keeps the communal space feeling fresh and bright.

A mix of window treatments can enhance the biophilic effects on a space, infusing a variety of natural textures and affecting how the sunlight moves through it. Bamboo shades, for example, leave behind a dappled light effect versus a more evenly dispersed light you'd get when using cotton. Additionally, you could consider top-down shades for privacy at the bottom of the window while still allowing sun to stream in through the top.

In some cases, the best dressed windows may be completely undressed, like in this utilitarian laundry room (bottom right) where the streaming sunlight makes the chore seem less daunting.

For sleepers who require a dark room for their beauty rest, blackout shades are best. Practically every window covering can be enhanced with a blackout backing that allows for total darkness as needed. When using these, though, make sure to consider the artificial lighting in the space and how you can use it to help maintain your circadian rhythm without the natural presence of the sun.

Layers of window treatments or none at all can certainly impact how a space feels.

Nature's Cue

See the Light

Our circadian rhythm is impacted by light and darkness and the rise and fall of the sun. The term "biodynamic lighting" refers to artificial light that can be adjusted to mimic natural illumination indoors. To maintain our circadian rhythm within our homes, we should consider adjusting the light based on the time of day. Morning light is invigorating, so look for bulbs that are bright and cool for the spaces you typically spend time in during the first part of the day. The redder light of the evening sun encourages our bodies to begin winding down, so opt for warmer bulbs in spaces where you spend the latter part of the day.

If you find that you use the same room(s) throughout the day, consider dimmers, which are an easy installation for any electrician. I install them on practically every light in my home. While they don't necessarily help me adjust the warmth of the light, they do modify the brightness. When my kids are doing their homework at the kitchen counter, I'll turn up the brightness to encourage focus. Then when I'm winding down at the end of the day, I'll dim those lights as I prepare for sleep.

Use sconces, pendants, chandeliers, and lamps to add beauty and dimension to a space and select bulbs that influence how you feel within it.

Layer Your Lighting

Illuminating your interior with artificial lighting in a biophilic way is sort of like baking a cake—it's all about the right mix of ingredients. A combination of complementary lighting styles will work together to create the most natural effect and enhance your space in the ways that will benefit your needs the most. Together, these layers create a harmonious, nature-inspired lighting scheme that feels restorative and dynamic. Let's work from the top down.

Overhead

In the absence of skylights or sun tunnels, warm, diffused recessed lighting can create a calming, natural glow. Use dimmers to transition from a strong daylight to a warm evening glow and completely shift the mood of the space. Pendants and chandeliers provide more visual interest while also illuminating the space.

Eye Level

At eye level, lighting adds practicality and connection to the human scale. Floor lamps, table lamps, and task lighting work together to illuminate functional areas while fostering a sense of intimacy in the space. These lights should feel warm and inviting, adding to the room's design without overpowering it.

Accent

Accent lighting is where your personality shines through. Think of undercabinet lights in kitchens or art lights that spotlight meaningful objects and textures. These small touches draw the eye in and bring depth to a room, mimicking the way sunlight plays on natural surfaces outdoors.

Uplighting

Typically reserved for outdoor spaces, uplighting can breathe life into interiors by casting dramatic shadows and accentuating indoor plants. Position an uplight near a tall plant to mimic the shifting interplay of sunlight and shadow found in nature.

Tip: When possible, prioritize natural light sources, as they highlight daylight's energizing qualities and help regulate our circadian rhythm.

PATTERNS of PORTUGAL
STUNNING
ICELAND
BEST DAY HIKES
VOGUE

Here, you can see recessed lights among the beams, pendants illuminating the island, directed under-cabinet lights over the work surface, and even lighting within the cabinetry.

Layered lighting contributes to the mood *and* function of a space. In this kitchen, gooseneck sconces not only provide visual interest above the open shelves, but they also illuminate what's stored on them.

Intention-Based Lighting Design

Lighting isn't just about seeing clearly—it's about shaping how we feel in a space. Whether you're trying to create a calm work zone, encourage connection, or set the tone for relaxation, the right lighting can make all the difference.

For Cognitive Ease

Ever notice how certain lighting makes it easier to focus, while harsh lighting just feels . . . off? That's because soft, diffused light helps reduce overstimulation in the brain, making it easier to process information and stay on task. Warm lighting even boosts serotonin, which naturally lifts your mood and helps you feel more at ease.

Diffused lighting helps your brain stay in a state of cognitive ease, leading to smoother and less overwhelming decision-making. While a harsh glare can be mentally exhausting, gentle, indirect light gives your eyes (and brain) a break, so you can focus and process information with less effort.

For spaces where you want to encourage focus—like a home office, reading nook, or even a cozy journaling corner—neuroaesthetic lighting (that which takes form and function into account) can make all the difference. The goal is to minimize glare and harsh contrasts, creating a setting that feels both mentally refreshing and visually comfortable. A mix of table lamps, natural light during the day, and dimmable under-cabinet or recessed lighting at night helps support concentration while still allowing for moments of relaxation.

opposite top: The texture of a paper lantern offers tactile engagement with the light source that enhances your experience with it.

opposite bottom: Directed light sources help direct focus on pathways or tasks.

For Emotional Regulation

For mindfulness practices, family time, or home workouts, dynamic lighting (lighting that shifts in brightness and color) can work wonders. Light influences the limbic system—the part of the brain that processes emotions—so small shifts in brightness and warmth can have a big impact on how we feel. Cooler light in the morning or during work sessions can enhance focus by stimulating dopamine production, helping you stay alert and motivated. In the evening, warmer lighting cues the parasympathetic nervous system to kick in, signaling your body to relax and unwind. Smart, color-tunable LED systems let you adjust the light throughout the day, naturally supporting your mood and energy levels.

For Engaging the Senses

Our brains crave sensory engagement—it's how we form memories, feel grounded, and create emotional connections with a space. When multiple senses are activated at once, the somatosensory cortex kicks in, reinforcing a feeling of comfort and presence. That's why textured lighting elements, like hammered metal, woven grass, or soft fabric shades don't just look beautiful—they actually help the brain's reward system light up, enhancing feelings of safety and relaxation. Studies suggest that tactile engagement helps regulate cortisol levels, lowering stress in high-stimulation environments. So, in spaces meant for deep connection—whether that's social gatherings or quiet moments of self-reflection—bring in lighting with textures that invite touch and familiarity.

CHEAT
EVERYTHING
A WILDERNESS OF ERROR
ERROL MORRIS
ELVIS COSTELLO

For Productivity

Lighting isn't just about aesthetics—it directly impacts how motivated and clear-headed we feel. Task lighting plays a huge role in productivity by stimulating the dopaminergic system, which helps boost focus and mental clarity. The right lighting setup can also reduce eye strain and prevent cognitive fatigue, keeping you sharper longer.

For high-focus areas like desks and workspaces, cooler, brighter light increases alertness and reaction time—perfect for when you need to be on your A-game. But productivity isn't just about intensity—it's also about adaptability. Modular lighting can shift as your needs change. Under-shelf LED strip lights above kitchen counters can improve visibility while cooking, while softer accent lighting during breaks helps ease visual strain, keeping you balanced throughout the day.

For Supporting Natural Patterns

Our bodies are wired to respond to natural light patterns—they help regulate our mood, energy, and stress levels. When we're exposed to shifting daylight, the visual cortex registers it as familiar, reinforcing relaxation and a sense of connection to nature. Indoors, you can re-create this effect by bringing in fixtures that mimic dappled sunlight, like perforated lamps that cast organic shadows similar to light filtering through tree canopies. This subtle play of light and movement has been shown to reduce amygdala hyperactivity, lowering stress and anxiety levels. It's a small but powerful way to make a space feel alive, rhythmic, and deeply calming.

In a moody office, heavy drapes help direct the focus to the task at hand.

Boost kitchen productivity with lighting that supports all kinds of tasks, from meal prep to homework.

Real-Life Lighting Lesson

In 2024, I had the opportunity to participate in *House Beautiful*'s Whole Home project, designing the "cocoon room" (aka basement relaxation space with zero natural light). Shadows and low light reduce visual input, calming the sensory cortex and signaling the brain to rest. Neuroscience shows that dim environments stimulate melatonin production—the hormone linked to relaxation and sleep—giving the mind permission to slow down, breathe, and focus inward. So shadows played a starring role in my design.

The combination of shadows cast by the swirled glass of the flush mount lights and the nearby perforated metal wall art (the white rectangles on either side of the sconces) created a sense of movement, texture, and depth that brought the room to life.

If you have a similar light-less situation, choose fixtures with textured or patterned glass to project unique shadows throughout the space. Experiment with light bulbs—softer, warmer bulbs enhance a cozy effect, while brighter ones sharpen the edges of shadows. Lastly, position your lights in spaces where you want to draw attention, like art or a focal wall. Align your choices with the room's purpose: playful shadows for energetic spaces and subtle light patterns for cozy or introspective rooms.

Establish Visual Texture

The custom metal wall art serves as a permanent shadow here, creating visual depth and acting as a grounding element on the wall. Its swirling pattern mimics the effect of real light and shadow, offering a sense of texture and layering even in dimly lit conditions.

Think of shadows as a design layer, much like color or texture. By pairing the shadows from the light fixtures with the artwork's visual depth, the cocoon room became more than just a functional space—it felt alive and emotionally engaging. The interplay of light and texture reinforced the restorative mood, aligning perfectly with the room's role as a sanctuary.

No natural light? Create shadow play with textured light sources.

How to Re-create this Effect

- Incorporate designs like metal screens, cutout panels, or perforated wall art to mimic shadow play seen in nature.
- Use contrast. Darker pieces against lighter walls enhance the visual shadow effect and vice versa.
- Place these elements in areas where light doesn't naturally interact to add balance and depth.
- Experiment! Move light sources or decor around to see how shadows work best with your space.

Previously, we talked about carving pathways for people to move between rooms. But those aren't the only pathways to consider—we should also think about how light is able to flow from space to space.

Here, the reflective stone surfaces and open-shelving room divider create a playground for light from the skylight and uncovered windows to bounce around in.

LOEWE
Urbänlike
Delicious Places
VOGUE
OCULUS

Mirrors and glossy paint brighten up this mantelpiece, even though it's painted in a dark charcoal shade.

In my own home, I keep my focus on maximizing the amount of light in each area. But your needs may be a little different. Biophilic design acknowledges the natural desire for both vast open areas and cozier spots for retreat (we'll dig into this more in a later chapter). We can use lighting to help achieve both. Be strategic with your design choices to help bounce or absorb light in visually interesting ways. Whatever your goal for the space, use light as a tool to help achieve that. You may want a dark and moody office to inspire focus or a light and bright breakfast nook for an invigorating start to the day.

For Instant Illumination

1. Opt for **metallic wallpaper or paint** with mica or pearl pigments, which add texture and interest while subtly enhancing the brightness of a room.
2. Consider **polished marble, quartz, or concrete** for flooring and countertops.
3. Choose glossy, glazed tiles for backsplashes or accent walls. **Zellige tiles** have an uneven, organic texture to them, so the glossy finish catches light in a particularly lovely way.
4. Create room dividers, wall treatments, or detailed insets on cabinets with **perforated metal panels** that disperse light in intricate patterns.
5. Incorporate **mother-of-pearl inlays** in furniture or decor for a lustrous effect.
6. Use pendant lights or chandeliers with **prismatic glass or crystal components** that refract and amplify light.
7. Opt for **textiles with subtle metallic threads** or silky texture for drapery, cushions, or upholstery.
8. Scatter light via a small **water wall or tabletop fountain** with LED lighting.

To Tone It Down

1. Absorb light with **velvet,** which creates depth and a moody atmosphere. Use it for furniture or curtains.
2. Choose **cork** for walls or floors. It not only absorbs light but also sound, making it functional and stylish for cozy spaces.
3. Use **matte clay or terra-cotta finishes** on walls or in decor for a soft, light-absorbing texture.
4. Add warmth with dark-stained or raw **wood elements.** Features like wood paneling, shiplap, or rough-hewn ceiling beams absorb light effectively.
5. Create visual weight in a room with **high-pile rugs** or rugs with multitextured designs.
6. Incorporate **natural fibers** like jute or seagrass for light-absorbing furniture pieces or wall hangings.
7. Go for **flat or matte paints** for feature walls to absorb light and create some drama.

In Light of Obstacles

We can often use light and creative design elements to solve pain points throughout our space. Here are a few examples:

If you've got awkward vertical space (in an entry or stairwell, for example), hang a mobile or cluster of lightweight sculptures to fill up the area in an interesting way. If you want to brighten that spot, opt for reflective materials like metal, acrylic, or glass. If you'd prefer to tone down the brightness there, choose something made of paper or wood instead.

Use frosted glass panels or laser-cut screens to diffuse natural light and create layered depth. This is a great option for, say, a bathroom window the neighbor could see into.

Install oversized canvases or hang textiles to absorb light and fill a large expanse of wall space. Refer to the previous page for a list of materials to consider based on what you're looking to achieve.

Brighten up a bookcase by installing reflective back panels (with antiqued mirrors cut to fit, perhaps) to combine function and light play.

Integrate LED strip lighting into alcoves or floating shelves to highlight objects on display and illuminate the more tucked-away zones.

Add dimension and fill vertical space by using lamps with large-scale fabric or parchment shades. They will diffuse light nicely and add a grounding element to the room.

Select large vases with reflective or matte finishes to reflect or absorb light as desired. These can be functional pieces that house greenery or standalone objects that infuse a new texture into the mix.

This chandelier is like jewelry for the room—the perfect finishing touch in a space with challenging ceiling angles.

Get Grounded:
RAISE A GLASS

It may seem like a simple thing, but, in reality, there are many variations and combinations of glass that can be used to enhance the vibe of a room and impact how light flows through it. Using the four seasons as my guide, I put together a few examples.

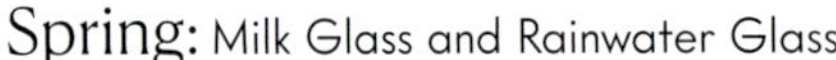

Spring: Milk Glass and Rainwater Glass

Imagine gentle spring rains, fresh greenery, and soft sunlight breaking through clouds. Get a similar effect with a mix of creamy, glowing light from milk glass pendants and the soft sparkle of rainwater glass.

Design Ideas: Pair milk glass pendants with brass or pastel finishes for a fresh and cheerful look. Use rainwater glass on sconces or table lamps to evoke the feeling of rain droplets catching light. Complement these with materials like linen or wood for an organic, spring-inspired feel.

Summer: Reeded Glass and Woven Pendants

Exude the vibrant, playful energy of summer with abundant light and natural textures.

Design Ideas: Reeded glass pendants capture the rippling effect of sunlight on water or a clear summer sky. Use rattan, wicker, or seagrass to enhance the casual, summery look. Alternatively use string lights with reeded glass bulbs to enhance outdoor gathering spaces with playful sparkle.

Fall: Amber Glass and Textured Shades

Like the golden warmth of autumn sunsets and the cozy richness of earthy tones, these elements offer grounding and comfort.

Design Ideas: Use woven or fabric shades in earthy tones like rust or olive green. Combine dimmable fixtures with amber tones to mimic the shifting light of autumn evenings. Brass or bronze finishes tie in beautifully with the rich colors of fall.

Winter: Frosted and Etched Glass

Inspired by the crisp stillness of snow-covered landscapes and the bluish-gray undertones of icy mornings, these glass types create diffused and textured lighting that evokes the calm and muted quality of winter light.

Design Ideas: Use frosted glass on pendants or sconces to soften light and mimic the brightness of snow. Accents of etched glass add subtle, frosty patterns reminiscent of ice crystals. Metallic finishes like chrome or brushed nickel will further enhance the reflective, wintry mood.

Plenty of sunlight + bright bulbs + crisp white paint + hints of metallic + polished stone surfaces = a luxe and vibrant cook space.

Light Bulb Moment

As with everything in biophilic design, your lighting is not a static element—it will constantly be evolving throughout the day. When you acknowledge this and work with it, you can set up each room to experience the most dynamic evolution as the lighting shifts. Bring in layers of artificial light to build off the natural light, play up the dynamic effects of shadows, and capitalize on the effects sunlight has on your body and your space. When we work with it rather than fight against it, lighting can become a powerful element in our design.

During the daytime, capitalize on the natural light streaming in through windows. As the sun goes down, strategically placed fixtures can take over the job.

Integrating Water Elements

I've always been drawn to the presence of water—it has this way of pulling me back into the moment, like a gentle nudge to slow down and just *be*. Maybe that's why I find so much comfort in simple rituals, like washing my hands when I'm feeling anxious. It's such an ordinary act, but the sensation of cool water running over my skin resets something inside me, almost like it's washing away the static in my mind.

Water isn't just essential for survival—our bodies are about 60 percent water, after all—but it also has a profound effect on our nervous system. Even without realizing it, we respond to water instinctively. Just drinking a glass of water, stepping into a warm shower, or even hearing the sound of rain can activate the parasympathetic nervous system, lowering our heart rate, reducing blood pressure, and helping us feel physically and emotionally at ease.

And here's the best part: You don't have to be *in* water to experience its benefits. The Blue Mind Theory suggests that simply being near water—whether it's a river, a fountain, or even an indoor water feature—can reduce anxiety, lower cortisol levels, and increase serotonin, boosting overall mood. The sight and sound of water have been scientifically linked to a sense of calm and clarity, which is why even a small tabletop fountain or a softly bubbling aquarium can bring a space to life in a deeply soothing way.

The presence of water—natural or manmade—can have a huge impact on our mood—both indoors and out.

With the tub situated in front of a window, bathers are encouraged to soak in the view. A skylight lets the sun shine in from above and enhances the texture of the grasscloth wallpaper and stunning stone work inside.

Beyond its calming effects, water represents movement, renewal, and life itself. Think about how it's constantly shifting—from evaporation to condensation to rainfall—a cycle that mirrors the ebb and flow of our own lives. In biophilic design, incorporating water elements like fountains, misting features, or even water-inspired artwork allows us to bring that natural rhythm indoors, making our spaces feel more fluid, connected, and alive.

Cultural Lesson

Water has consistently been more than just a resource—it's a symbol of renewal, purification, and connection across cultures. From ancient traditions to modern rituals, people around the world have recognized the power of water, weaving it into their daily lives in meaningful ways.

Ancient Egyptian Civilization

The Nile River was central to Ancient Egyptian life and worship, symbolizing rebirth and sustaining agriculture. The annual flooding was considered a divine act that renewed the land's fertility.

Chinese Philosophy

In Taoism, water is a metaphor for flexibility and strength. The Tao Te Ching describes water as the softest yet most powerful force, capable of wearing down rock over time.

Hinduism

Rivers like the Ganges are considered sacred, embodying purity and spiritual renewal. Ritual bathing in these waters is believed to wash away sins.

Indigenous Beliefs

Many Indigenous people view water as a sacred life-giving force, often tied to ceremonies and storytelling that emphasize balance and respect for nature.

Roman Aqueducts

These marvels of engineering highlight the ancient Romans' deep understanding of water's necessity for life, hygiene, and prosperity. The aqueducts symbolized civilization and progress.

Islamic Gardens

Designed as earthly representations of paradise, Islamic gardens prominently feature water in fountains, pools, and canals, symbolizing abundance and the divine.

Immersion in warm water increases blood flow to the skin and activates the parasympathetic nervous system to lower heart rate and blood pressure. Open the windows to let in nature sounds that further quiet the amygdala (your brain's stress center).

The Cleansing Power of Water

From baptism rituals to ceremonial washes and spa therapies, water is seen as a way to cleanse both body and mind—marking a fresh start. Leverage this symbolic power in your home, too. Create a ritual of renewal by incorporating simple water elements. A facial mist can refresh your skin while offering a sensory reset. Pair this with a sound machine that plays calming water noises—whether it's a gentle rainstorm or a babbling brook—and you've transformed an everyday space into an oasis of tranquility.

Flow and Emotional Release

Just as rivers carry away debris, flowing water serves as a powerful reminder to release emotional clutter. By incorporating water features within your home, you're creating a space that facilitates letting go of stress and negativity. Channel the therapeutic benefits of water even in your everyday chores. When you're working by the kitchen sink or washing machine, repeat mindfulness mantras or affirmations, transforming what might feel like a mundane task into a ritual of emotional release. It's a simple practice that recharges your mind and spirit—a win-win!

Renewal Through Hydration

On a physiological level, water is essential for replenishing and rejuvenating our bodies. Just as staying hydrated refreshes us, incorporating water into home design—whether through drink stations with infused water pitchers or humidifying features—supports physical and emotional well-being.

The stone trough situated beside a wood slat wall and a bounty of bushes creates an ideal biophilic setup to capitalize on the cleansing effects of water.

The Great Equalizer

Water is both calming and powerful, reflecting the balance we seek in life. It can soothe as a still pond or invigorate as crashing waves. Incorporating water into your home can help balance chaotic energy with tranquility. Use contrasting water features, like a bubbling fountain alongside a reflective sound bowl, to symbolize the yin-yang balance of movement and stillness.

Water's Connection to Homeostasis

In the body, water helps regulate temperature and deliver nutrients. In the home, water can play a similar role, bringing balance to the sensory environment. For example, the sound of water reduces auditory clutter, masking harsh sounds and creating an atmosphere of peace. Visual elements like water walls or aquariums provide focal points to ground the space. Install a water feature near a high-traffic area, such as the entryway, to balance the hustle of daily life with a regulating presence.

A Mediator of Energy

In feng shui, water is tied to wealth and flow, symbolizing prosperity and balance. Incorporating water strategically can direct the energy flow in your home to create a more harmonious environment. Place a small fountain in the living room or a reflective bowl near a window to symbolize abundance and draw energy inward.

Consider how you can enhance the experience of the standard water elements in your space (faucets, tubs, showers, spigots). This setup seamlessly blends into the natural space thanks to the rough texture of the basin, the arch of the spout, and the climbing greenery growing alongside.

Our brains react to asymmetry, so odd numbers are pleasing to the eye. Here, three patinaed water spouts provide that off-kilter element that provides satisfaction.

A teak tub provides a relaxing smell when the steam from the hot water connects with it, creating a multisensory experience for relaxation.

This bathroom expertly incorporates stone and tile in a way that is soothing yet still visually appealing. The repetitive patterns and neutral colors add texture and interest without becoming overwhelming.

Upgrade What Already Exists

Showers are standard in most homes, so consider how you might be able to amplify what's currently there. Swap out a builder-grade showerhead for a rain shower version or one that offers aromatherapy, for example. The most recent technology even allows users to enjoy a luxurious bathing experience while keeping water conservation top of mind. Typically, this is done through aerators or flow restrictors, which offer the feeling of strong water pressure while regulating the flow.

I'm more of a bath person myself but aim to make conscious, sustainable choices at the same time, so I limit the luxury as much as possible. Occasionally, I'll prepare a hand or foot bath when I need a pause for a mindful, water-saving activity. If you do bathe, consider ways you might reuse the bathwater. When using chemical-free, biodegradable products, reuse the water for nurturing plants or cleaning outdoor spaces. You could even use it to pre-soak clothes before running a laundry cycle.

Take It Up a Notch

If you have the luxury of being able to make more structural upgrades, consider a wet room (where the tub and shower are contained within a fully waterproof space). Or if you've got pups, a pot filler is an ingenious addition to a feeding station. No longer just for prepping spaghetti, this fixture can make the daily chore of filling those pet bowls a bit easier. A more budget-friendly option would be to incorporate a fountain water bowl that offers your pet freshly cycled water to drink and gives you the benefit of the trickling sound. These enhancements acknowledge the impact water has on our daily routines and makes them even more enjoyable.

Soak in the View

Our experience with nature happens through all five senses. The sight of water—near or far, real or abstract—can infuse a soothing sensation. Highlight the view of a lake, river, ocean, or even simply the rain out of a window. Alternatively, incorporate artwork that depicts some kind of water element.

Get Grounded

STIMULATE ALL 5 SENSES

Sight

The Blue Mind Theory, coined by marine biologist Wallace J. Nichols, maintains that proximity to water induces a meditative state, enhancing calmness and creativity. Do this by simply incorporating a photo of water from a memorable trip or adding some sort of visible water feature into your home.

Smell

Water features like fountains or waterfalls increase humidity, improving air quality and reducing issues like dry skin, irritated eyes, and respiratory problems. According to the American Lung Association, optimal indoor humidity levels of 30 to 50 percent prevent dryness and help alleviate symptoms of asthma or allergies.

Sound

The sound of water, like flowing streams or waves, activates the parasympathetic nervous system, which lowers heart rate and reduces stress. Indoor water walls, tabletop fountains, or aquariums can replicate these stress-reducing effects. People report heightened feelings of relaxation, focus, and happiness when near water.

Tactile tiles reminiscent of river rocks amplify this shower stall's biophilic impact.

Touch

Cold water immersion has been shown to reduce inflammation and muscle soreness, aiding physical recovery. While full immersion might be impractical, incorporating chilled water basins or foot baths at home can offer similar recovery benefits.

Taste

Adequate hydration maintains electrical activity and neurotransmitter balance in the brain. Studies show that dehydration can impair cognitive performance, including memory, focus, and alertness. A sleek filtered-water dispenser or built-in tap encourages mindful hydration. Create a designated station with fruit and herb infusions (think mint, lemon, or cucumber) to make hydration even more appealing.

Find Your Own Way

Repetition hammers home a new idea, right? So I'm going to remind you again that when it comes to introducing biophilia into your space, you don't have to go all or nothing. Start where you're at and implement small changes into your room or your routine.

Notice the large aquarium behind the dining table. While not everyone has the space or budget to install a built-in option like this, take inspiration from it and search for a tabletop version for your home (something as simple as a fishbowl will do!). The movement of the water and interaction with the creatures inside bring a space to life.

My Biophilic Blueprint is the ocean, so water plays a big part in the visualization of that. Every morning, I turn on a YouTube channel that streams live tropical views and sounds and keep it on in the background for the first hour of my day. I set this escapist atmosphere to center myself and prepare for the day's work ahead of me. Search for water elements that remind you of your own Biophilic Blueprint to reap the same benefits.

The custom blue cabinetry and fish wallpaper above the wet bar extends the feeling of the aquarium across the entire wall, adding to its impact in the space.

opposite: Similar to how a rug can help define zones in an open floor plan, so, too, can a patch of tile in a large exterior space. Here, it highlights the outdoor shower.

above: Even small spaces can sustain water features. Here, a plunge pool sits alongside a pond to create an aquatic space that benefits both body and mind.

In this oasis of local landscaping, an infinity pool reflects sunlight during the day and the stars' glow at night.

The Universal Connector

Leonardo da Vinci famously described water as "the driving force of all nature," reflecting its vital and unifying role. Water is a powerful symbol and tool for renewal and balance. By understanding its qualities and aligning them with how we want to feel at home, we can create spaces that foster healing, harmony, and vitality. Incorporate artwork that evokes the feeling of water, textures that replicate the look (like bubble glass), or more overt representations throughout your decor.

However you're able to invite water into your view from your home—whether a backyard pool or a simple fountain—it's worth it. Water's presence can slow the mind, calm the body, and restore balance.

People have used water in healing rituals since practically the beginning of time. Japanese onsen (or hot springs) and Finnish saunas highlight water's rejuvenating properties, and modern wellness trends, like hydrotherapy, trace their roots to these ancient traditions. Consider how you can bring elements of these rituals into your home.

Water has been a life force for centuries, of course. Wall-mount faucets are my favorite design nod to ancient baths in Italy.

Natural light, a mixture of rough and polished stone, and the warmth of the wooden vanity combine to create an ultra-organic bathing experience.

Nature's Cue
Take the Plunge

Cold-plunge pools are all the rage right now, but they can also come with a steep price tag. Rather than making any big-ticket purchase to get the benefits of an ice bath, I've started adjusting my morning shower routine to stimulate my body in the same way. I start my day with a cool shower (right around 70 degrees—nothing too extreme) to wake me up and activate alertness.

Meanwhile, when I'm winding down at the end of the day, or if I'm having an anxiety episode, I'll make use of warm water to help relax my body's fight-or-flight response.

You can take advantage of the benefits in any way that works for you. Start by reducing the temp of your morning shower or bath to as low as you can tolerate and see how that affects your senses.

above: Bathing outdoors is a parasympathetic supercharger that layers thermal therapy of warm water on top of nature therapy. It provides tactile, visual, auditory, and olfactory stimulation.

opposite: Shade trees enhance an outdoor water retreat—and those that bear fruit are an added bonus!

To Your Health!

People who live near bodies of water (like oceans, lakes, or rivers) have reportedly lower stress levels and increased physical activity, leading to better overall health. Indoor water elements, even in urban settings, mimic the calming effects of being near natural bodies of water.

Mood Enhancement

Moving water generates negative ions, which are molecules believed to increase serotonin levels and reduce symptoms of depression. Studies in environmental psychology show that observing repetitive natural processes, such as flowing water, has a meditative effect.

Sleep Aid

A study in *Sleep Health* found that white noise, including water sounds, significantly reduced sleep onset time and increased sleep depth. Try placing a small fountain or water wall near the bedroom or setting up a sound machine to encourage restful slumber.

Emotional Detoxification

Flowing water is a metaphor for letting go of emotional clutter, encouraging a mindset of renewal and change. Incorporate small reflective pools, wall-mounted waterfalls, or even a bowl with floating candles indoors to support moments of mindfulness.

Boundary Setting

Use water to delineate areas of your home based on how you want to feel in each space—peaceful, creative, or social. For example, a reflective pool can create a sense of introspection, while a lively water fountain can energize a family gathering area.

Even the ripply appearance of glass can allude to the movement of water in your interior.

Ways to Add Water Features

The bathroom is an obvious spot for incorporating water therapy, but what other spaces in your home might benefit from it as well? The living room often sits underutilized, serving more as a showpiece than a functional area. By rethinking this space and incorporating zones for water therapy, it can become a retreat for relaxation, creativity, and emotional balance. Water elements—whether physical or sensory—can be integrated into different areas of the room to create a versatile, restorative environment. Bedrooms might also benefit from the implementation of a few of these ideas.

A Reading Corner for Peace and Meditation: Place a small water fountain on a side table near a cozy chair, soft lighting, and a basket for books or journals. The gentle trickle of water promotes peace and mindfulness, making the reading corner ideal for quiet reflection. The sound can also act as a mental boundary from the rest of the house.

A Waterfall Wall as a Focal Point: Above the sofa, install a waterfall wall or use rain glass as an accent. The visual movement of the water or light reflecting off the glass can become the centerpiece of the room, drawing attention and setting a calming tone. Watching water flow provides a meditative experience, helping to soothe overstimulated minds and encourage relaxation.

Speakers for Multisensory Connection: If physical water features aren't feasible, use speakers (Bluetooth ones will do) to play gentle water sounds throughout the room. Choose playlists with ocean waves, flowing rivers, or soft rain sounds to evoke the presence of water. Soundscapes can create the illusion of water, connecting you to its soothing properties and balance.

The sculptural quality of a fountain is a great decorative addition to a space, while the movement and sound of the water within is ultrasoothing.

Aquariums or Terrariums of Any Size for Therapeutic Benefits: Incorporate an aquarium or terrarium—whether a small desktop option or a large built-in installation—and position it where it will be visible from the main seating area, encouraging interaction and reflection. Watching aquatic or botanical life can reduce stress, lower blood pressure, and create a sense of tranquility.

Rain Chains by Picture Windows: The rhythmic qualities of water, whether from waves or rain, are inherently soothing. They tap into our biological need for predictable patterns, providing comfort and reducing anxiety. Hang decorative rain chains near large windows to mimic the cascading effect of water. Even without rain, they can function as art pieces. Place stones or plants beneath the chain to enhance the biophilic nature of the design.

Mist and Humidity for Wellness: Use ultrasonic misting devices or humidifying fountains to add a subtle, fog-like effect. These elements improve air quality while also creating an ethereal ambience. Add in essential oils like eucalyptus or lavender for extra aromatherapy benefits. Balanced humidity not only enhances comfort but also supports respiratory health and creates a spa-like atmosphere.

Pour It On

H_2O is the substance that makes our bodies and the earth function, so by intentionally incorporating it throughout our home, we can maximize our well-being within the space. Use water features to foster an environment of calm and relaxation as well as a reminder to let go of emotional burdens and make room for fresh starts. Plus, combining sight, sound, and touch, water elements help ground us in the present moment, reducing stress and encouraging mindfulness.

above: Even a small bathroom can become the ultimate sanctuary when using biophilic design to enhance an intentional mindfulness routine. The lush wallpaper, animal artwork, and combination of natural materials create an inviting space.

opposite: Brass fixtures add brightness that complements the reflective quality of water.

Creating Natural Order

A major component of biophilia incorporates the idea of "prospect and refuge"—basically our biological desire to access a vast expanse of possibility while having secure spots where we can retreat. The example that came up multiple times in my research was an animal on the savanna. They can explore the wide-open landscape to hunt (prospect) while naturally keeping an eye out for a safe haven to rest (refuge).

We can learn from this wild example and incorporate a similar outlook within our homes. While we might find satisfaction in an open floor plan that allows us to see much of the living space, there is something to be said for creating spots for retreat as well. It could be a cozy corner to escape to for some quiet reading time or a nook under the stairs in the dining room to stash serving supplies. Storage and organization can reinforce the feeling of refuge because when things are put away, we feel grounded and safe. Creating these small spaces is all about intentionality.

Additionally, biophilic design maintains the importance of "complexity and order" within a space. Each area should feel rich and layered, yes, but also not cluttered or in a state of disarray. To me, the key to making each zone feel lived-in and balanced is to layer pattern on pattern, texture on texture, and incorporate feel-good elements. Yet we should do so in a way that remains organized and gather inspiration from nature wherever we can.

In nature, transitions between landscapes often appear seamless. Trees give way to meadows and rivers move across valleys. The same is true in a well-designed home. Using our chosen Biophilic Blueprint as inspiration across adjoining spaces creates visual flow while allowing cozy layers of color, texture, and pattern to shine.

Window seats, alcoves, and storage cubbies can all provide a sense of refuge within the home.

upper-left: Consider a limewash wallpaper for the natural look without the mess.

upper-right: Any space—no matter how small—can benefit from a faux or low-light plant. It's the perfect biophilic finishing touch.

bottom: A curved built-in maximizes seating and makes the architecture feel protective and enveloping.

Choose Sustainability

Opt for vintage or secondhand furniture. The life these pieces have lived before entering your space will add richness and texture while also being a more sustainable choice than something brand new or flimsy that will need to be replaced in a few short years.

Mix Materials

Just as you would find a mix of materials and textures along the seashore, blend a variety of elements throughout your space to create an instant feeling of comfort. Seagrass, bouclé, linen, limewash, brass, birch, rattan, clay, leather: All of these elements can be made to work together in a way that feels rich and lived in. Relying too heavily on a single material can leave a space feeling one-note.

Forgo uniformity in favor of a blend of finishes and a creative use of all the space you have available. Here, the dark island cabinetry references nature's shadows while the combination of white uppers and floating shelves lends an open and bright feel.

Maximize Every Inch

Let no corner or niche go overlooked. Each is an opportunity to create intentional landing spots for yourself or your stuff. Consider that awkward spot under the stairs as an opening for organization or an area that can support your daily rituals. I've used these nooks as out-of-sight drop zones near an entryway or stylish pet retreats with a comfy bed, built-in feeding station, and storage for their essentials.

Larger spots like bay windows, dormers, and built-ins may provide the perfect area for a cozy cocoon that keeps you feeling safe and enveloped. The tactile sensory experience of sitting within these spaces will help your body relax into that authentic and vulnerable state where you feel most secure. If your space doesn't have obvious spots for refuge, carve them out! With just a few simple elements, you can create an inviting place for respite. If you are in a position to add built-ins (like banquette seating in a dining nook), I constantly advise my clients that the investment will provide some of the best value for their money. Built-ins feel instantly inviting and allow you to use a potentially awkward space so much more effectively. By offering these spots of structure and security, we create opportunities for retreat without completely detaching them from the rest of the home, maintaining that desired sense of connection.

opposite: Cozy upholstery tucked against a limewash wall, warm wood, and a textured rug creates the perfect biophilic corner to unwind and reset your body and mind.

Real-Life Storage Solution

In a client's home, we transformed an unused vertical niche in a high-traffic common area outside the primary bedroom into a sleek and functional family command center. Initially, the client was concerned about the complexity of adding power here, but we were able to easily pull electricity from the existing outlet below to create built-in USB ports and additional outlets. Now this once-overlooked space serves as a practical and stylish device turn-in station, where the kids can "check in" their phones and tablets each night to earn screen time for the next day.

Why It Works

The charging station encourages healthy digital habits while offering a clutter-free solution for busy mornings and evenings. Plus, beyond charging devices, the niche now serves as a family hub for organization and storage. Pulling electricity from the nearby outlet proved to be a straightforward and budget-friendly way to enhance the space without major renovations.

Pro Tip

Cord organizers and concealed charging docks keep the area looking neat and streamlined.

Step away from your devices (at least overnight) and identify a technology drop zone.

Layered rugs, pillows, and throws in a variety of textures make this space feel ultracozy. The assorted colors, variety of finishes, and subtle patterns throughout the room add to the warm and inviting effect.

Global Influence

As a Chinese American, I have found the principles of Taoism and feng shui to be foundational to my upbringing, teaching me to live in harmony with nature and to honor the flow of energy within a space. Taoism emphasizes balance and flow, often described as "wu wei"—a sense of effortless action that mirrors the natural rhythms of life. In a biophilic space, this translates into designing environments that feel seamless and intuitive, where nature and structure coexist harmoniously without force or rigidity. Similarly, feng shui, rooted in Taoist principles, focuses on qi (energy flow) and how the arrangement of objects and spaces can influence our well-being. Arranging furniture to ensure clear pathways or incorporating elements like water, wood, and earth into a room design can enhance the energy and create a calming, restorative environment.

I had relatives who lived in Japan as well and they'd send me cards, art, and little trinkets that helped shape my sense of design as I grew up. For example, Japanese philosophies like wabi sabi celebrate imperfection and find beauty in the natural wear and patina as a result of time. This perspective invites us to embrace the organic textures, irregular forms, and unique character that nature brings into our spaces.

In many ways, these traditions form the foundation of my belief that nature isn't just something we look at—it's something we bring into our spaces, our hearts, and our lives. By weaving these influences together, we can create environments that are not only visually beautiful but deeply restorative, honoring the balance between imperfection and harmony.

These cultural influences have guided my personal design philosophy and have created the foundation for my outlook on biophilic design. We will dive deeper into some of these ideas to gather specific takeaways that you can incorporate into your home. You may find that your own personal heritage or cultural experiences reveal other ways to explore the benefits of biophilia.

My mother's vintage Chinese rosewood furniture and antique treasures reflect our family's heritage, while plants, metallic elements, and other modern decor pieces help to infuse a well-rounded biophilic design.

Nature's Cue

Appreciate the Blemishes

Look around you and identify the "flaws" in your space and materials used. Is there a knot in the wood on your flooring or coffee table? What about the veining of a countertop or patina on a brass bowl? These are all examples of the environment's impact on a material that influences how it appears over time. While much of modern architecture and design would put that in the cast-off pile, those with biophilia and wabi sabi in mind embrace these imperfections as a gentle reminder of the living, breathing world around us.

Textured walls, rough-hewn beams, and handmade tile lend a sense of comfort thanks to their irregularity.

Everything in Its Place

While biophilic design feels like a modern approach to creating spaces that enhance well-being, its roots share striking similarities with ancient rituals like feng shui. For thousands of years, feng shui has emphasized harmony and balance by arranging spaces to optimize qi. Similarly, biophilic design seeks to foster harmony by reconnecting us to nature through thoughtful design.

In both approaches, placement plays a critical role. Feng shui's principles of positioning furniture to enhance energy flow are mirrored in biophilic concepts like prospect and refuge—the idea of creating spaces that feel both open and secure. For example, positioning seating to face a window with a view of nature (prospect) while ensuring it's against a solid wall for protective backing (refuge) offers both psychological comfort and a sense of grounded energy. This balance encourages relaxation, focus, and well-being.

opposite: The wooden mirror, stone planter, and rattan tray are simple ways to bring nature into a bathroom.

right: While this space doesn't strictly follow traditional feng shui, it naturally integrates core principles of intentional biophilic design: Mossy green walls remind us of the earth while blue bedding nods to the calming flow of water.

From my perspective, feng shui is about creating intentional spaces that break up stagnant energy and foster a positive flow. By integrating these principles within biophilic design, we can enhance the way a room feels and functions. For instance:

Energy Breakers

Feng shui often suggests placing furniture or plants in areas where energy feels "stuck." In biophilic terms, this could mean using greenery to liven up dark corners or placing a soft rug to ground a large, open space. So how do you know when energy is stuck? You can *feel* it. It's that part of your home where you hesitate to spend time, the corner that always seems cluttered, or the area that just doesn't feel inviting.

Zoning with Nature

Feng shui uses screens or partitions to define spaces, which aligns with biophilia's use of natural materials like wood dividers or tall plants to create zones without disconnecting them from the room as a whole.

Light and Flow

Both practices emphasize the importance of natural light and clear pathways. A clutter-free path with good lighting invites energy to flow freely and makes a space feel alive and welcoming.

Balancing Rest and Engagement

At the heart of feng shui is the concept of yin and yang—the interplay of opposing forces that create harmony. Yin represents calmness, softness, and restfulness, while yang embodies energy, brightness, and activity. Biophilic design mirrors this balance by blending quiet, restorative spaces with dynamic and engaging ones. We need both restorative and energizing spaces in our home. Too much stimulation can feel chaotic, while too much calm can feel uninspiring.

Think of your home as a rhythm rather than a formula. Some rooms—like a bedroom or a reading nook—should lean into *yin* qualities, with soft textures, cozy lighting, and soothing colors that invite rest. Others—like a kitchen or a living room—benefit from a *yang* boost, with dynamic layouts, natural light, and lively colors that energize and engage.

Even within a single space, you can strike a balance. A laundry room, often seen as purely functional, can become a *yin* retreat with warm wood shelving, soft lighting, and beautifully organized baskets that bring a sense of ease. Meanwhile, a dining area can lean *yang* with bold trim, statement lighting, and plants that add life and vibrancy.

By blending biophilic design and feng shui, we create homes that aren't just beautiful—they feel right. Spaces that support both our need to recharge and our need to engage. It's about shaping our surroundings with care and purpose, making every room work *with* us, not against us.

opposite: Fresh greenery (like a trailing vine or vase of blooms) acts as an energy breaker to soften the harsh lines of a space. Biophilic elements like this can shift the mood and instantly make a room feel more dynamic.

above: Pretty and soothing decor can help make the occasionally daunting task of laundry more bearable. Functional? Yes. Inviting? Definitely.

Get Grounded

LAYER WITH INTENTION

A space feels most inviting when it is full of thoughtful elements meant to add richness and depth. Use this biophilic layering checklist to ensure your home is full of just the right amount of complexity:

COLOR

Choose a complementary palette inspired by your Biophilic Blueprint and incorporate those shades on your walls, furniture, textiles, and accessories.

PATTERN

Mix large-scale statement motifs (like on the window shades opposite) with small-scale accents (the upholstery and cushions).

TEXTURE

Incorporate natural, tactile materials like wood, linen, clay, or jute.

FORM

Go for organic, curved lines, which soften a space and reflect the irregular lines found in the natural world.

BIOPHILIC ELEMENTS

Add a sensory connection to the space with plants, natural light, or water-inspired decor.

Notice the cohesive palette, varying pattern scales, and bounty of florals that adorn this space.

Here are just a few examples of how you might incorporate different elements from your Biophilic Blueprint to make your home feel warm, inviting, and inspired by nature.

Ocean-Inspired Connection

Color: Pale blues, seafoam greens, and soft grays combined with driftwood beige and pearly whites

Pattern: Wave-like tile or subtle blue-gray walls with nautical striped linens or a textured rug

Texture: Smooth ceramic finishes, gauzy linen window coverings, and driftwood-inspired shelving paired with pebble trays or polished stone accents to add tactile depth

Biophilic Elements: Small water feature or bowl of polished stones to bring water's calming essence indoors; mirrors to reflect natural light and evoke the expansive quality of the ocean

Meadow-Inspired Connection

Color: Creamy whites, pale greens, and soft yellows pair with dusty salmon pinks or muted lavender

Pattern: Botanical-inspired wallpaper or a large-scale floral textile with a delicate floral or striped cushion on an accent chair

Texture: Linen textiles with woven rattan furniture and a braided jute rug for tactile warmth

Biophilic Elements: A small vase of wildflowers and trailing ivy on a shelf, sheer curtains that mimic meadow breezes

Desert-Inspired Connection

Color: Main base of sandy neutrals and terra-cotta tones with a secondary layer of deeper clay, rust, or sage-green accents

Pattern: Terra-cotta-colored area rug with a Moroccan motif combined with woven or striped rust and beige throw pillows

Texture: Smooth, adobe-inspired walls or matte paint layered with rough clay vases, woven jute rugs, and soft linen curtains

Biophilic Elements: Cacti or succulents, arched doorways to enhance natural light, sheer curtains in warm tones to mimic the desert glow

Mountain-Inspired Connection

Color: Deep forest green and brass with stone-like cream shades and misty blue-green accents

Pattern: A plaid or oversize herringbone weave paired with a subtle gray and white stone with marbled veining

Texture: Dark wood furniture, matte black fixtures, and wool or felt textiles

Biophilic Elements: A fiddle-leaf fig or potted fern for greenery, vertical open shelving with moss-inspired decor or plants, tall indoor plants to echo the upward pull of a forest canopy

A cohesive color palette, geometric textiles, varied natural textures, plenty of curved edges, and an assortment of plants give this desert retreat tons of character.

Think Like a Painter

You know how the famed art teacher Bob Ross would guide his viewers to paint idyllic landscapes? He didn't just dive in with happy little trees—he started with the horizon line, layered in the background, and built depth and texture with each brushstroke. Let's apply that same thoughtful process to designing interiors and create spaces that feel layered, textured, and deeply inspired by nature.

Step 1: Establish your horizon line. Just like in a painting, this is where the eye naturally rests—it's the anchor of the room. Whether it's a fireplace, window, TV, or artwork, this focal point sets the tone. Start here and design outward.

Step 2: Build your ground layer. This includes everything from the floor up to waist height: rugs, sofas, coffee tables, and baskets. Like the earth in a landscape painting, this layer grounds the space.

Step 3: Fill the middle zone. The waist-height area is where function meets design. Console tables, stools, and plants add variety and balance, bridging the lower ground layer with the upper elements.

Step 4: Layer the upper third (the sky). The top section brings depth and personality. Pendant lights and chandeliers draw the eye upward, while a painted or wallpapered ceiling completes the space.

Step 5: Add perspective (foreground, middle ground, background). The "foreground" might include a statement chair or a striking centerpiece. The "midground" could feature functional and decorative elements like side tables or greenery. The "background" fades into subtler tones and textures, such as wall colors or details like wainscoting, trim, or curtains that provide balance and harmony.

Step 6: Embrace texture and happy accidents. Bob Ross famously welcomed "happy accidents," finding beauty in imperfection. In design, this translates to personal touches that bring authenticity to a space—like a slightly weathered table, a handmade vase, or a well-loved rug.

Step 7: Blend and smooth. In painting, blending softens edges, creating a seamless transition between elements. In design, use rugs to define spaces, large windows to connect indoors with outdoors, or soft lighting to tie elements together and maintain flow.

Step 8: Add lighting. This is like the final brushstrokes in a painting—it highlights the details and brings everything to life.

Step 9: Step back and reflect. Each element should feel purposeful and connected. Inspired by nature's complexity, a well-designed room feels textured, layered, and alive, yet also restful and balanced—just like a Bob Ross painting.

The busy wallpaper in the adjacent dining room provides visual interest to the background, so the foreground can be kept more subdued with white walls and neutral foundational elements. An architectural sconce and warm textiles add tons of personality.

The (Nearly) Imperceptible

The most powerful aspects of design are often the ones you don't immediately notice. Our brains are naturally drawn to things that feel incomplete, sparking curiosity and anticipation. Ever noticed how a door left slightly ajar or a staircase that disappears around a corner ignites your curiosity? These subtle design choices activate your prefrontal cortex, keeping your attention focused and heightening your sense of discovery.

This is where sub-perceptual design comes in—elements so subtle they almost go unnoticed, but still influence how we feel. Think of the soft texture of a plastered wall or the slight change in material underfoot as you step onto a rug—these details guide your focus and influence your emotional state without you consciously realizing it. Research has shown that these tiny cues activate the brain's default mode network, which governs creativity, mindfulness, and the feeling of being "in the flow."

Good design creates intrigue, allowing mystery to unfold. A space doesn't need to shout for attention; rather, it can invite exploration through layers of subtlety. This kind of design generates emotional depth, letting the unseen enhance the seen. The anticipation and the unknown creates a richer, more compelling experience, engaging us on a deeper level.

The biophilic elements you include in your space do not have to be in-your-face but can (and should) include subtle nods to nature.

Woven window treatments are my go-to choice to add visual interest and texture (not to mention function) into a bedroom. Just like in nature, you can find so many different varieties of colors and styles to choose from.

Add In Organization

On top of being thoughtfully designed, each space should be organized. That doesn't just mean "a place for everything and everything in its place." It's also about making the room feel cohesive and well thought out. There may be lots of stuff, but it's all intentionally placed. There may be a variety of colors, but they should all feel inspired by your Biophilic Blueprint. Purposefully made decisions play a big role in how a space is perceived. Here's how to pull all of these aspects together.

Simplify

Universal Organizing Rule

Clear clutter first to create space in a room, closet, or pantry.

Biophilic Connection

In nature, space creates calm—like open meadows, clear water surfaces, or sparse desert landscapes. Use "visual breathing room" as a key principle.

In Practice

- Store items that function together in the same area to simplify and create easy access.
- Use neutral or natural-colored containers (woven baskets, glass jars, wooden trays) to enhance calm rather than add to visual chaos.

Categorize

Universal Organizing Rule

Sort items into groups by function, size, or frequency of use.

Biophilic Connection

Fractals—repeating patterns found in leaves, seashells, or snowflakes—are deeply calming because our brains seek order often found in nature. In organization, categorizing generates this same natural rhythm.

In Practice

- Group items by task or function, like clothes by color or pantry goods by food group.
- Use multiples of the same containers, bins, or dividers to create a visual pattern of order.

Smart organizational strategies can help reduce the cognitive load and feelings of stress because you'll always know where to find something.

Contain

Universal Organizing Rule

Use containers to hold and manage smaller items, creating limits and reducing clutter.

Biophilic Connection

Prioritize natural materials that offer tactile and visual comfort (wood, linen, ceramic, or woven fibers). These help ground us and create a physical connection to nature.

In Practice

- Replace plastic bins with woven baskets, ceramic trays, or reclaimed wood boxes.
- Use soft linen organizers for drawers or closets instead of synthetic dividers.

Layer

Universal Organizing Rule

Layer items with intention, keeping frequently used pieces neatly organized while on display.

Biophilic Connection

Nature creates layers in ecosystems—like forest floors, tree canopies, and tide pools. Mirroring these layers in organization creates depth and balance.

In Practice

- Use tiered shelves or risers to layer goods in a pantry or medicine cabinet.
- Stack containers vertically, mimicking how plants grow at different heights.

Prioritize Flow

Universal Organizing Rule

Arrange spaces for ease of movement and visibility. Make frequently used items easy to access while disguising clutter.

Biophilic Connection

Nature balances prospect (open visibility) with refuge (sheltered spaces).

In Practice

- Open shelves or clear containers create visual "prospect" (you can see what's there).
- Closed drawers, baskets, or cabinets create "refuge" for items you want hidden but still accessible.

Create Beauty

Universal Organizing Rule

Organized spaces can be beautiful *and* functional.

Biophilic Connection

Elements like plants, water features, or natural light elevate an organized space into a restorative one.

In Practice

- Add a small faux plant on a pantry or closet shelf or hang organic wallpaper or art.
- Position organized spaces near natural light when possible. Sun tunnels work wonders for illuminating these areas.

opposite: From the geometric design on the back of the bookshelf to the detailed drawer fronts on the window seat, this corner provides tons of storage and tons of character.

STILL
LIVE BEAUTIFUL

Get Real

When we use our Biophilic Blueprint as our guide and thoughtfully introduce both decorative and practical elements, we not only create beautiful rooms, but also establish spaces that encourage peace and connection—a hallmark of biophilic design. That just-right balance of a well-thought-out space invites a feeling of harmony and supports well-being within the home. When we feel truly at ease, we help our bodies relax into an authentic state where we feel most safe and secure.

Incorporating a balance of textures, patterns, and cultural influences will ultimately make a space feel most harmonious.

Lean into large windows: A built-in bench with secluded storage brings order and functionality to the space, while the proximity to the view brings peace of mind.

Living Outside

Fresh air provides mental clarity. The act of breathing it in has a nearly immediate calming effect. In fact, studies have shown that spending just five minutes outside reduces cortisol levels (aka our stress hormone) and increases endorphins. Plus, as we've already explored, exposure to natural elements like sunlight, plants, and water boosts serotonin levels, improving mood and promoting emotional balance. The Japanese practice of shinrin-yoku (forest bathing) highlights how even brief contact with nature can lower blood pressure and anxiety. Ultimately, improved oxygen intake leads to better brain function and energy, so stepping outside even for a minute can counteract the stuffy air of indoor spaces.

Growing up, I spent countless days wandering outdoors, whether it was picking dandelions on walks with my sister or exploring the wild fields behind our houses. Those moments weren't just a pastime—they were a lifeline. As adults, it's easy to forget the simple joy of stepping outside when our lives revolve around screens and endless to-do lists. Working from home, I have come to understand just how vital it is to have intentional outdoor spaces that invite us to unplug and recharge.

But creating a habit of going outside takes more than good intentions—it requires good design. Without a space that's attractive and accessible, it's all too easy to stay cooped up indoors. Whether it's an inviting spot set up outside your home's front window or a patch of greenery that catches the morning light, having an outdoor area that's thoughtfully planned makes all the difference. These small, intentional spaces turn the simple act of stepping outside into a daily ritual that nourishes the mind-body connection.

There's no easier way to incorporate nature into your surroundings than by creating a spot to sit among it. An elevated platform provides a clear view of the landscape.

Establish a Daily Outdoor Routine

Start your day with a trip outdoors, even if just for a quick moment while sipping your coffee or tea. Throughout the day, take breaks outside between tasks or meetings to clear your head. Use these occasions to stretch, breathe deeply, and reset. To encourage an al fresco respite under the stars at the end of the day, add a reclining chair or beanbag along with soft lighting as a comfortable place to unwind.

Promote a Sensory Experience

Rain chains, wind chimes, bird feeders, and birdbaths provide an enhanced sensory element to the outdoor experience, while encouraging wild visitors and adding soothing sounds.

Get Fired Up

Fire adds warmth and ambience and creates a natural gathering spot. Some areas have restrictions on open fires, so check with your local municipality for rules. Small tabletop firepits are ideal for tight spaces (opt for gas or bioethanol options for clean-burning flames). Alternatively, arrange battery-operated LED candles or lanterns for cozy, flickering light that mimics a campfire without the work.

Use a hammock, firepit, or water feature to encourage interaction with the outdoors.

Lean into Small Spaces

Balconies and patios are ideal for vertical gardens or railing planters. You can also just open a window, add a hanging planter nearby, and create an inviting nook to lean out of.

Take a Seat

Functional and comfortable seating options throughout your exterior space will encourage you and your guests to linger there. Hammocks and swing chairs offer a relaxed, playful vibe and can be installed even in small spaces. In particularly narrow spots, built-in seating can double as storage for garden tools or cushions. For ultimate convenience, lightweight folding chairs and tables can be rearranged or tucked away as needed.

Multiple seating styles will help maximize whatever outdoor space you have and provide a variety of options for how to interact with it. A hammock makes the experience more introverted, while a sofa encourages interaction.

jeremy fox
on vegetables
pasta

Biophilic design encourages breaking down barriers between indoor and outdoor spaces for a seamless transition that enhances the beauty and functionality of your home. Thoughtfully designed outdoor areas can serve as extensions of your living space, providing spots for relaxation, socialization, and recreation.

The Biophilic Backyard

As with your indoor space, it's important to consider what natural elements you're exposing yourself to within your outdoor oasis—whether that's a backyard or balcony. Plants, water features, animal motifs and habitats, and natural materials are hugely beneficial both indoors and out.

Native Plants

Choose plants that are indigenous to your area to support local wildlife and ensure sustainability.

Water Features

Install fountains or ponds to introduce the calming sounds of water and enhance relaxation.

Wildlife Habitats

Create spaces that attract and support local fauna to foster a dynamic and lively environment. Bird feeders and butterfly gardens are great options, as are bee hotels, frog ponds, and even hedgehog shelters.

Natural Materials

Opt for wood, stone, and other natural materials in your outdoor structures and furniture to create a cohesive and organic aesthetic.

GARDEN

This once bland and unused side yard has become my secret French garden where I sit to journal or just enjoy the breeze.

We covered in previous chapters how biophilic design for indoor spaces considers opportunities for rest and retreat as well as intentional pathways between spaces. We can apply these same concepts to our outdoor space to enhance our experience of nature.

Shade and Shelter

On sunny days, adjustable options like umbrellas and retractable awnings keep things cool and flexible. Want something more permanent? Pergolas and trellises not only provide shade but also invite a touch of nature. Add climbing plants like ivy, wisteria, or morning glory for a lush, green canopy. For those drizzly afternoons, outdoor curtains or transparent panels can keep you comfortable while still feeling connected to the outdoors.

Intentional Pathways

Guide movement through your outdoor space with thoughtful pathways. Encourage exploration by using stone or gravel to lead to a specific spot like a bench or garden bed. Use decorative stepping stones in smaller areas to add charm and practicality. Even a few wooden planks of a deck or boardwalk can create a visual cue to step farther outside and enjoy Mother Nature.

Use stepping stones, pavers, or wooden planks to help navigate your outdoor space and maximize your interaction with every inch.

Sure, your outdoor oasis can (and should) be a place of peace, but it can also encourage movement and appreciation for the natural world by facilitating a spot for games and activities. Consider these more interactive features:

Outdoor Games

Incorporate simple lawn or tabletop entertainment like bocce, cornhole, or chess (keeping an eye out for those made of wood, stone, or another natural material to enhance the space's biophilic attributes). Additionally, consider installing a chalkboard or mural wall for kids and adults to keep score—bonus: They can also use it to express their creativity.

Art and Sculptures

Add a personal touch with outdoor sculptures or even DIY art pieces that reflect your personality (and perhaps infuse a bit of your Biophilic Blueprint here as well).

Seasonal Displays

Create a rotating decor area with seasonal touches like pumpkins in the fall, string lights in winter, or vibrant flowers in spring to once again encourage engagement with nature.

A trellis of climbing greenery can help provide visual interest to an otherwise boring side of a building. It's like living art.

A Place to Gather

If you love to entertain and have outdoor space to spare, carve out room for a table and chairs and surround it with lush greenery. When you're dining in nature, you don't need any decor for the meal to feel divine.

A Potting Station

If you love to garden, set up a spot where you can pot up your favorite flowers and plants with a simple outdoor stand. Let it act as a beautiful display when not in use.

Fragrant lavender, a hedge of gorgeous hydrangeas, a soothing water feature, and flexible shade near these lounge chairs enhance the multisensory experience of this outdoor space.

Go Native

While I encourage you to create your indoor oasis in the landscape style that speaks to you most, when considering your outdoor design, let the natural surroundings guide you a bit more. Basically, don't fight nature. If you live in Santa Fe, a lush meadow retreat might not be in the cards. Believe me, I had to learn this the hard way.

Years ago, I wanted the look of lavender near my front door, so I planted purple salvia (which looks similar, but is not the same at all) to line the walkway leading to our porch. Little did I know that this particular plant grows extremely fast and is like catnip to bees. In a matter of weeks, these wispy shrubs had grown into huge bushes that were vibrating with insects. I'd invite friends over for playdates and these poor people had to sprint through the hive I'd inadvertently created and hope they didn't get stung. They laughed it off, but I was mortified.

Point being, opt for native plants when possible, but do your research. Talk to local native nurseries for advice and map out your plan in advance. In doing so, you can infuse some themes into your outdoor space to make it more enticing. Try one of these options based on what will thrive in your area:

Zen Garden

Combine smooth stones, sand, and a minimalist water feature to create a meditative retreat. Add bamboo screens or small bonsai trees for a calming, Japanese-inspired aesthetic.

Desert Escape

Enhance stucco, stone, and clay features with decor pieces in similarly neutral tones. Amp up the vibe with cacti in terracotta pots, a grounding rug in a complementary blue shade, or rattan garden stools (for extra seating or to accommodate snacks).

Parisian Paradise

Combine reclaimed wood furniture, vintage planters, and dusty tones for a cozy, European feel.

Select native plants that will thrive in your area while incorporating other elements that complement your Biophilic Blueprint.

Go ahead and get your hands dirty—it's good for you! Interacting with the earth can reduce stress, encourage movement, and promote mindfulness.

Dig In

Gardening isn't just about tending plants—it's about nurturing yourself. It encourages physical activity, which boosts your mood and strengthens your immune system. Consider incorporating one of the following garden styles into your outdoor space to reap these benefits.

Container Garden

Perfect for small patios, balconies, or even windowsills, container gardens are a great way to add nature's beauty into practically any space. Use vibrantly colored pots or upcycled containers to give your garden extra personality and charm. What's great about container gardens is that if one plant doesn't make it, the investment is small, and the effort to replace it is minimal—no guilt or commitment here! The flexibility of containers lets you easily change things up, giving you the freedom to experiment with new configurations. It's a perfect choice for beginner gardeners or anyone who likes a little variety (like me!). Plus, you get to enjoy the satisfaction of watching your plants grow without the long-term upkeep of a permanent garden.

Edible Garden

Turn your home into a farm-to-table haven by growing simple greens, strawberries, or cherry tomatoes. Whether you have a raised bed, vertical planter, or just a few containers, these offer an easy way to utilize your green thumb and stay engaged with your greenery. Plus, there's nothing more satisfying than picking fresh produce you've nurtured yourself.

Pollinator Garden

Create a buzzing, vibrant plot that attracts bees, butterflies, and hummingbirds with colorful flowers like marigolds, sunflowers, and bee balm. Not only will you invite nature's energy to your space, but you'll also help support local ecosystems.

Rock Garden

If you're looking for a low-maintenance option, a rock garden is the way to go. By using stones as the foundation and planting hardy vegetation in between, you can create a stunning, effortless oasis that works in any space, regardless of the size. This option is perfect for those who want a natural, zen feel with minimal upkeep and watering.

Zone Out

Maximize the opportunity to spend time outdoors by creating the most multifunctional area possible. Consider how you could incorporate different zones to serve all your needs: lounging, dining, grilling, potting plants, and/or playing. I always encourage creating flexible spaces that can seamlessly transition from one use to another or do double duty. Think about using swivel seating, versatile folding screens, or a statement outdoor rug to define spaces within your outdoor retreat.

While your greenery style may be limited by your location, your decor is not. Implement the same techniques we discussed for your interior as you bring together your outdoor space. Incorporate a mix of outdoor-friendly natural materials (some may need to be specially treated to weather the elements), motifs related to your Biophilic Blueprint, and thoughtful lighting to create a space that you want to spend time in as you commune with nature.

Create zones in your outdoor living space just as you would inside. This not only maximizes functionality but also simplifies the vast sensory stimulation our environment might supply.

How to Create Visual Definition

- Consider **multilevel platforms or decking** to subtly define zones without walls or barriers.
- Use **sturdy screens** to create privacy or separate one space from the next. Opt for screens made from metal, bamboo, rattan, or outdoor fabric panels. Bonus points for those that can easily be stored when not needed. If your screen of choice is more permanent, consider attaching planters to it for additional visual depth and connection to nature.
- Large, **weather-resistant rugs** can anchor and define zones. Choose patterns that complement your aesthetic while adding warmth and comfort underfoot.
- A **daybed or hanging swing bed** can serve as a cozy escape for reading or napping but can also function as additional seating during get-togethers.
- **Portable firepits and heaters** help create a comfortable atmosphere and act as a natural gathering spot.
- **Pergolas with adjustable louvers or retractable shade sails** provide shade and give you flexibility, allowing the space to be used on hot, sunny days.
- **Foldable bistro sets** are perfect for small spaces and can be easily stored or rearranged to accommodate different functions, from casual coffee breaks to intimate dinners.

Nature's Cue

Solar Spotlight

Designing a backyard with native plants and natural materials fosters local wildlife, supporting ecosystems and promoting biodiversity. Incorporating natural elements can also help reduce energy consumption by providing natural shade and cooling, decreasing the need for artificial climate control. Additionally, an outdoor space is an ideal spot to harness the power of the sun. Consider some of these solar-powered upgrades for your exterior space:

The sun is an integral part of most exterior spaces, so harness its power for improved circadian rhythm, increased productivity, and lower eye strain.

1. **Water Features:** Many retailers offer solar fountains and birdbaths that prevent stagnant water.
2. **Umbrellas:** Available from many popular retailers, these shades often come with USB ports and built-in LED lighting.
3. **Charging Stations:** Keep your tech powered up in an eco-friendly way.
4. **Pergolas or Gazebos:** These are increasingly common and customizable. Pergolas with built-in solar panels for lighting and electricity are sold by specialized eco-friendly brands or can be custom-designed.
5. **Outdoor Kitchens:** Solar-powered appliances like mini-fridges, stoves, and LED lights for outdoor kitchens are available, but they often require portable solar panels or integrated systems.
6. **Pathway Markers:** Solar bricks or pavers may need to be sourced from specialized suppliers, but solar-powered stake lights are widely available.
7. **Greenhouses:** These are common in sustainable gardening and offer fans or lighting that are powered by solar panels.
8. **Art or Sculptures:** Garden statues are popular and provide ways to incorporate even more nature motifs into your exterior space. Now you can find illuminated options that do double duty of adding to the ambience and lighting up the space.
9. **Outdoor Shades or Awnings:** These are increasingly available as smart-home technology evolves.
10. **Outdoor Entertainment Systems:** Portable solar panels or kits can power projectors, lights, and speakers. These systems are often DIY and very achievable.

The firepit is clearly the heart of this outdoor oasis, but the woven chairs add biophilic texture. Their tactile surface and breathable construction soften the hardscape, making the outdoor lounge area feel grounded, human, and alive.

Create a Holistic Retreat

Designing a multisensory outdoor space is a fantastic way to transform your surroundings into a refuge that engages all five senses.

Sound

Celebrate the calming sounds of nature. Hang wind chimes, line pathways with rustling grasses, or use gravel to create satisfying crunches underfoot. Pipe in sounds of birds, waves, or wind through outdoor speakers, enhancing the tranquility—especially to help mask unwanted noise like traffic, trains, or construction.

Scent

Fill the air with the fragrances of nature. Plant lavender, jasmine, and mint near seating areas to add soothing aromas. Herb planters not only provide wonderful smells, but they're also practical additions to have within reach of the kitchen.

Touch

Texture is key for a grounding experience. Think smooth pebbles, warm wooden furniture, and plush outdoor cushions. If you're looking for something extra, create a small sand or gravel area for barefoot walks or mindful raking exercises.

Sight

Lighting sets the mood, so add solar-powered string lights, lanterns, or LED candles to create a soft, magical ambience. Mirrors and reflective surfaces can amplify natural light, making any space feel more expansive. And, to keep things feeling organic, let climbing plants cover unsightly elements like sheds or trash can housing, blending the natural with the practical.

Climbing plants can provide a lovely scent while also helping to disguise the more inorganic elements in our outdoor space.

Get Grounded

FACILITATE QUICK BREAKS

Creating a retreat space isn't just about having a place to sit; it's about giving yourself a reason to step outside. Place a small garden bag by your chair, ready for quick tasks like pulling weeds or pruning a bush. This way, you're not just idly sitting there, you're engaging with your surroundings and reaping the benefits of light activity. A quick break with purposeful movement can be just as refreshing as a short brisk walk.

When you consistently engage in a task in the same space, your brain reinforces the connection, making it easier to start and continue the activity. This creates a healthy habit loop where each positive action supports the next, continuously feeding into your well-being and creating a home that nurtures you physically and mentally.

If gardening isn't your thing, try stepping outside for a quick photo walk—snapping pictures of anything that inspires you—or queuing up a favorite podcast. The point is to create a small habit loop that gets you outdoors and reconnected, even for just a few minutes.

Adjusting window coverings creates active participation in the intention of bringing life into your interiors.

Nature's Cue

Fresh Take

The simple act of breathing in fresh air can help remind us of life's natural flow, release tension, and reconnect with our bodies. That mental pause, no matter how short, can act as a reset, allowing us to approach tasks or challenges with fresh energy and perspective. For me, taking care of my well-being means intentionally breaking out of my routine. It can be as simple as opening the windows in the morning to let in the crisp air or breaking up the monotony of meetings by taking the dogs out for a quick walk. On weekends, I open all the windows in the house while cleaning to circulate the air, refreshing both the space and my mindset. I've even assigned Natalie, my youngest, the chore of pulling up and down the living room shades each day—a task that helps her develop habits that send happy hormones to the body. These small, intentional acts remind us to reconnect with the natural world, whether we step outside or invite it in.

Blur the Lines

If we don't thoughtfully design our homes with access points that encourage us to engage with the outdoors, we simply won't do it. As creatures of habit, we need intentional visual cues—beautiful French doors, expansive sliding glass panels, or a well-placed window—to entice us to connect with nature. There's something undeniably romantic and invigorating about opening a door and feeling that first whoosh of fresh air fill your lungs or standing by a sunlit window with the clear light warming your face. It's these small yet powerful moments that foster a sense of hope, positivity, and connection with the world outside. I strive to bring that sense of wonder and opportunity into my clients' homes.

Many clients initially feel that adding a new window or door is an overwhelming construction project or unnecessary expense. But I've found that once they experience the transformation—both aesthetic and emotional—they realize it was not only feasible, but life-enhancing.

I once worked with a client who had a small, awkward wall in their dining area facing the backyard. They had always assumed that adding French doors would be too expensive and disruptive to their daily life. After working through their concerns and showing them how accessible the project actually was, they decided to take the plunge. The results were incredible. That once-forgotten corner became their favorite spot in the house, enabling morning coffee outside, impromptu family dinners under the stars, and a newfound sense of connection to their outdoor space. The light that poured into their home transformed not just the room, but also their daily habits and mood. It was absolutely worth it in the end.

Set up a seating spot nearly anywhere to make the most of the space you have.

Whether it's a Juliet balcony off a bedroom, a small window overlooking a garden, or a grand set of French doors leading to a patio, I believe in designing for possibility. These elements don't just open up spaces physically—they open up our lives to new experiences, fresh air, and the joy of simply being in tune with nature. I encourage my clients to embrace these ideas, knowing that the reward far outweighs the perceived challenges.

A well-placed window or door isn't just an architectural feature; it's an invitation—to step outside, to embrace new habits, and to find inspiration in the everyday. If it's simply not in your budget to add a window or door, highlight the features that currently exist to make the most of what connection they do offer to the outdoors.

Unify your indoor and outdoor living areas with a cohesive color palette and design style. When the doors are thrown open, there's almost no boundary between the two.

The Call of the Wild

When we consider not just our own needs, but the needs of other living beings around us, we can create spaces that foster that connection and enhance the overall biophilic effect. Highlighting natural elements and inviting wildlife to share the setup provides an even richer experience.

Use natural motifs on window treatments to enhance the view or choose a bold wildlife wallpaper to infuse nature into a windowless space.

following spread: Just as the seasons lead to change in nature, so, too, do the needs of our home. This layered space might foster reflection today and morph to facilitate conversation down the line.

505

505

Embracing the Evolution of Home

There's a universal truth in nature, in therapy, and in design that we're never truly "done." As we evolve and transition into each new season of life, whether we realize it or not, our needs and tastes shift along with us. Learning to embrace each phase and adapt our surroundings accordingly is key to feeling at peace within our homes.

I remember when my eldest daughter, Rachel, went off to college. It was a bittersweet transition—one that left me feeling both proud and wistful. The absence of her daily presence created a noticeable void, with one fewer body moving through the halls and one less voice at the dinner table. There were moments when I would catch myself feeling the weight of it, sitting in the hallway loft where she and her sisters used to do their homework, letting the warmth of a sunbeam remind me that this change, too, was a good one. Rachel was blossoming in her own space now, carving out a life for herself. And, back home, we were doing the same.

With her departure, our home evolved to meet our new needs. Her bedroom, once filled with high school mementos and dreams, became a flex space for calls and meetings during the day and a guest room when other family visited. My youngest daughter finally got the bathroom she had always longed for—a space to call entirely her own. My middle daughter no longer had to share her bedroom. Instead, she moved into what was once my mom's space, as her visits became less frequent and we found ourselves traveling to her more often instead.

Be open to shifting your space around as your needs change. Your home is meant to evolve!

The biggest shift, however, was reimagining the heart of our home. We swapped our dining and family rooms to create a mini great room where we could gather, lounge, and connect more comfortably. Our old family room, once brimming with toys, baby swings, and playpens, is now a multifunctional dining area that also serves as my podcast recording space. The shift in layout reflects our evolving needs—what once was a hub for toddler chaos is now a place of meaningful conversation and creative expression.

And that's the beauty of it all. Our relationship with our homes will never truly arrive at a final destination. Like the constant flow of nature, our homes will evolve to reflect where we are currently in life. It's what I tell my clients and remind myself every day: There is no perfect design or ultimate relationship with our spaces. It's a continuous transformation, a journey of striving toward our most authentic selves in each season of life.

Let's look to nature as a therapeutic tool to guide us through these transitions. Living mindfully and in harmony with the earth, we become more grounded and more capable stewards of our lives and planet. Start small with intentional changes—swapping a room's function, introducing new habits, or simply embracing a bit more light—and watch how these shifts can have a profound impact on mood, energy, and the spaces we inhabit.

The proven benefits of incorporating biophilic design into our living spaces should encourage us all to embrace this constant evolution. By bringing elements of the outdoors into our homes, harnessing the power of water and light, layering with intention, and maximizing our time spent outdoors, we can cultivate a home that not only adapts to our needs, but enhances our well-being through every stage of life.

This dining room could easily transform into a lounge later on with a quick furniture swap. The built-ins provide a grounding element that can be styled differently to suit the needs of the space.

Mixed materials in warm neutral tones plus artwork and patterns that allude to nature make this plush seating area ultra-inviting for a family.

Design for Right Now

This grand entry provides a clear path in and through the house, with multiple zones for different functions situated along that path.

So as we engage with our spaces, let's continue to consider how we can incorporate nature, get inspired by it, and interact with it in ways that align with our current needs.

In the entryway, we may want a welcoming and hard-working landing spot that invites family members and guests to stay a while. How can we make it engaging and practical to draw people in and away from the door?

- Add a natural-fiber rug (like jute or sisal) mixed with cozier fibers to ground the space with texture and durability along with welcoming softness.
- Incorporate seasonal live branches or a vase of fresh flowers to create an inviting focal point that reflects the changing seasons.
- Use a wooden bench or console table to introduce warmth and provide functional storage.
- Install a mirror to reflect light and evoke the openness of the outdoors.

The living room is typically a more social zone where we aim to foster connection and comfort.

- Arrange seating to encourage communication, such as placing chairs in a circular or semi-circular layout.
- Incorporate a mix of natural materials, like a reclaimed driftwood coffee table or a leather pouf, to add warmth and textural variety.
- Layer the space with cozy throws or pillows in seasonal patterns and tones. This creates a grounding sense of calm by mimicking the rhythms of nature.
- Add large potted plants to corners of the room that are too small or narrow for any functional piece of furniture. These provide an instant connection to the outdoors.

In an open floor plan, a variety of light fixtures helps distinguish between areas. Here, an undulating woven pendant invites diners to the breakfast nook.

In the kitchen, we aim to enhance functionality and connection while inspiring creativity ("What *will* I cook for dinner?").

- Use open shelving to display ceramic dishes or glass jars filled with pantry staples tailored to the season. For the holidays, feature items like flour, sugar, and festive treats; for summer, showcase colorful spices and barbecue rubs. This not only reflects the abundance of nature but also brings visual interest and functionality to your cook space.
- Create a compact herb garden by hanging small pots from a tension rod mounted across a kitchen window or wall. This setup incorporates greenery while being highly practical—simply snip the herbs as needed for cooking. The added benefit? The fresh scents provide natural aromatherapy, making the kitchen a more inviting and refreshing space.
- Repurpose leftover countertop materials, such as marble, quartz, or wood, into custom cutting boards or trivets. This approach is not only sustainable but also ensures these functional pieces seamlessly match your kitchen design.
- When possible, position a large window or skylight to flood the kitchen with natural light or keep window curtains open as much as you can. This enhances the sense of connection to the outdoors, while also boosting energy and mood during meal prep or family cooking sessions.

Bedrooms are typically reserved as a refuge for comfort and revitalization.

- Utilize ethically sourced, reclaimed wood for flooring, nightstands, and shelves. The unique grains and textures of these materials add character and help create a soothing environment.
- Enhance the biophilic atmosphere by incorporating a variety of indoor plants, driftwood, branches, and other natural elements. These additions bring life and organic beauty into the space.
- Consider casement windows with divided lites that can be easily screened or opened, giving you the ability to adjust airflow and connect with the outdoors, as the seasons allow.
- Refresh your walls with low-VOC paint. A simple coat of breathable, nontoxic paint in a soft, natural tone—like warm taupe, sage green, or misty blue—can transform your space while keeping indoor air quality clean and healthy. Introduce natural scents for a sensory experience. Linen sprays, essential oil diffusers, or a small bowl of dried lavender or cedar chips can help set the tone for restful sleep.

Wood, linen, and leather work together to create a cozy sanctuary you just want to sink into. The panoramic windows provide all the artwork this space needs.

HSD

In bathrooms, we often aim to create a soothing, spa-like spot that refreshes and restores with the infusion of natural elements.

- Add humidity-loving plants like rabbit's foot ferns, orchids, or begonias to soften the space and enhance air quality.
- Use natural materials such as bamboo or teak for bath mats, shelving, or stools to bring in warmth and texture.
- Incorporate stone accents on the shower pan or floor of a wet room.
- Install a rain showerhead to mimic the calming sensation of gentle rainfall.
- Enhance the ambience with dimmable lighting for a serene, spa-like atmosphere.
- Add speakers for a multisensory experience.
- Include natural scents like eucalyptus or lavender through dried plants or essential oil diffusers.

Vine-like wallpaper and a bud vase with a sprig of fresh florals help transform this bathroom into a biophilic retreat.

The office is a spot where we want to promote productivity and focus while reducing feelings of stress.

- When possible, arrange the desk to face a window and capitalize on natural light or a view of greenery for moments of visual rest.
- Add a live plant to the work surface to reduce anxiety and improve air quality.
- Use natural wood tones throughout the space to create a grounded, calming aesthetic.
- Hang artwork or photography of natural landscapes to evoke the restorative effects of the outdoors.

The kids' room is where we want to create a calming space that still encourages creativity and activity.

- Use bright, nature-inspired colors like sunny yellows, grassy greens, or sky blues to spark imagination.
- Incorporate soft, natural materials on play mats and cushions to create a safe and cozy environment.
- Safely secure a climbing plant or add playful wall decals of trees and animals to introduce nature motifs.
- Include storage made of wicker or wood to organize toys while maintaining a natural, earthy feel.

Kids' rooms don't need to look like a rainbow, and office spaces don't have to feel stoic. Let their natural beauty shine and highlight the elements that inspire you most.

YOU

And our outdoor space is where we can extend the home's living area and promote a direct connection to nature.

- Create zones for dining, lounging, and play using outdoor rugs or natural stone pavers to define each area.
- Add string lights to mimic the stars and create a cozy ambience for evenings.
- Incorporate native plants to support local wildlife and create a low-maintenance, natural landscape.
- Use a water feature, like a small fountain or birdbath, to incorporate the soothing sound of water.

Garage doors provide the ultimate indoor/outdoor living experience. As the weather permits, throw them open and take your coffee outside.

Keep It Neat

When each element is thoughtfully and purposefully introduced, the overall effect tends to be most impactful. Maintain the good vibes by implementing smart organizational strategies that keep these elements tidy with biophilia in mind. Use this checklist:

1. **Simplify:** Clear clutter and leave space for visual breathing room.
2. **Categorize:** Group items into categories for natural rhythm.
3. **Contain:** Use natural materials for storage (think woven, wooden, or linen options).
4. **Layer:** Arrange items on a shelf from front to back with the tallest toward the rear.
5. **Prioritize Flow:** Create open visibility (prospect) and tucked-away storage (refuge).
6. **Create Beauty:** Incorporate plants, natural light, and organic textures for sensory richness.

A shelf, a tray, or a vase of crocheted flowers helps provide clear boundaries for your stuff and minimize visible clutter.

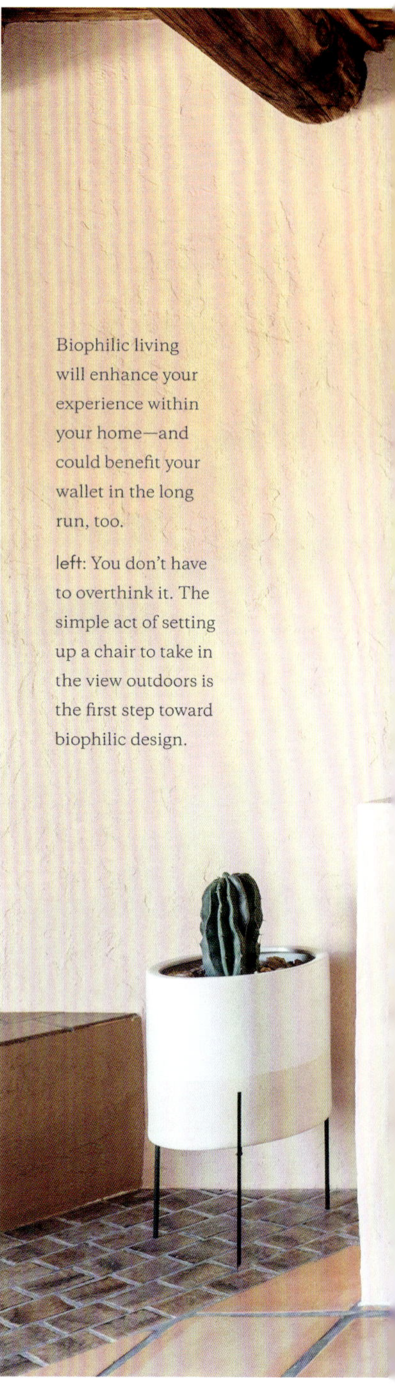

Biophilic living will enhance your experience within your home—and could benefit your wallet in the long run, too.

left: You don't have to overthink it. The simple act of setting up a chair to take in the view outdoors is the first step toward biophilic design.

L.A. MODERN

Be a Force of Nature

When we harness the power of the world around us and build spaces that help us evolve into our best selves, we maximize our well-being within our homes. Biophilic design allows us to capitalize on the things that earth organically provides us and to become better stewards of the planet.

So what are you waiting for? Step outside. Take in the textures, colors, and imperfections of nature. Bring them home—not just in the way you design, but in the way you live. Let your home be a safe space that breathes, a place that heals. Because when you create a home that nurtures you, you become a force of nature in your own right.

Let your space nurture you.

Resources

Biophilic & Quiet-Luxury Home Textile/Decor Resources (AAPI + Organic + Sustainable)

AAPI-OWNED / SUPPORTED AND DESIGNED

- Tantuvi—Hand-loomed rugs and textiles, natural dyes, Indian master weavers. Architectural Digest darling. www.tantuvistudio.com
- Minna—Organic cotton and wool textiles, plant-based dyes. www.minna-goods.com
- Morrow Soft Goods—Founders have Asian heritage; sustainably made bedding and throws in linen, organic cotton. https://morrowsoftgoods.com

ORGANIC / BIOPHILIC-ALIGNED QUIET LUXURY

- Coyuchi—Organic cotton bedding, GOTS-certified, earth-tone palette. www.coyuchi.com
- Sefte Living—Alpaca, organic cotton, and silk blends; supports female artisans globally. www.sefteliving.com
- de Le Cuona—Handcrafted organic linens, textured neutrals, understated luxury. https://delecuona.com/

Decor & Accent Sources

HEATH CERAMICS—CALIFORNIA-MADE TABLEWARE AND TILE WITH NATURE-INSPIRED GLAZES

- Fireclay Tile sustainable and recycled materials
- Rejuvenation planters and outdoor living
- The Sill
- ABC Carpet & Home—Conscious sourcing, natural fibers, artisan-made pieces

Acknowledgments

To my editor, Angelin—your expertise, keen eye, and thoughtful guidance have been unsurpassed, helping me refine and shape my vision of biophilic design into something both relatable and life-changing.

To everyone at Clarkson Potter who touched these pages—including Marysarah Quinn, Natalie Blachere, and Kim Tyner—thank you for helping me bring this vision to life.

I'm deeply grateful to my championing agent, Kim Perel, for their steadfast belief in this book, and to my brilliant writer, Stephanie Sisco, who helped shape and clarify my vision of biophilic design as a pathway to the belief that therapy is home. Your steady, unwavering support has meant the world to me.

Credits

To all the designers and photographers who contributed to *Grounded Living*, thank you for bringing your vision, creativity, and heart to this book. Every space and image reflects not only your artistry but your shared intention to connect people with the restorative power of nature. Each contribution added depth, warmth, and meaning, shaping *Grounded Living* into more than a book. It became a collective expression of what it means to live in harmony with our surroundings.

I'm deeply honored to share your talents here, and grateful for the spirit of collaboration that made this possible.

PHOTOGRAPHERS

DESIGNERS, ARCHITECTS, AND STYLISTS

Index